Shirley Temple

Robert Windeler

W. H. Allen · London
A division of Howard & Wyndham Ltd
1976

PRINTED AND BOUND IN GREAT BRITAIN BY
THE GARDEN CITY PRESS LIMITED, LETCHWORTH,
HERTFORDSHIRE SG6 1JS
FOR THE PUBLISHERS, W. H. ALLEN & CO. LTD,
44 HILL STREET, LONDON W1X 8LB

ISBN 0 491 01524 0

Shirley Temple

FOR THOSE ARTISTS AND ENTERTAINERS
WHO ALSO WORK HARD TO MAKE
A BETTER WORLD

Preface

In 1972 and 1973 as a consultant to UNICEF at the United Nations, I organised concerts in Europe by well-known American pop singers, and wrote and produced television and radio public service spots using volunteer actors and entertainers—all to raise money to help the children of developing nations. To be able to combine the sometimes frivolous aspects of show business and the always serious needs of the developing nations seemed to me unusual, useful and fun, and it was all three. But throughout my two years in and around the U.N. I was repeatedly made aware of someone who had preceded me in coming from Hollywood to the United Nations—at first as a near-laughing stock—and who had done and would continue to do far more dedicated and lasting work. I already admired her for that, and although Shirley Temple Black and I weren't to meet until the summer of 1974 at her home in Woodside, California, it was while working with UNICEF that I first thought of doing this book.

Her childhood films had all been before my time and by the time she came back to television in her storybook anthology I was in high school and both too old and too young for fairy

7

tales. I knew, as a writer about movies, that hers were totally unimportant in the history of cinema or the planet—except collectively as a box-office phenomenon. (What I didn't know until later was that she'd be the first to agree with that judgment.) But Shirley Temple's era—1933–1940—was in many ways the most interesting and productive in American movies in general, and it happened to begin at the precise moment that Mary Pickford, the subject of my previous biography, had retired. Selfishly, that meant I could continue my education in the history of American cinema right up until the time—just after Shirley Temple's teenaged and adult movies ending in 1949—that I started going to Saturday matinees myself, and when child stars were already a thing of the past.

But the chief reason for, and the real emphasis of, this book is Shirley Temple Black, survivor. Her unique childhood and the money she made during it would have made any withdrawal from society she chose almost understandable. But as wife, mother, volunteer, amateur politician and—incongruous as it may have sounded several years ago—international diplomat, Shirley Temple Black has been a positive, constructive human being who has done much to help her fellow human beings. An illness and operation that had been traumatic for millions of women before her she faced with calm bravery and turned it into a positive experience for millions of others. I don't necessarily endorse her politics or other philosophical positions, but I do endorse—and I hope celebrate—her zest for life and for tackling the problems of now and the future, particularly the use of our natural resources.

I'm grateful to UNICEF for expanding my horizons and to the United Nations family for giving Shirley Temple Black the first international channels for her considerable energies. Many individuals were helpful to me in the researching of this book, and I'm particularly grateful to Jane Withers, former Senator George Murphy, the late Robert Graham Paris, Allan Dwan and Buddy Ebsen for their memories of little Shirley. Jim Eason of KSO-FM in San Francisco and Lisa Trumpler of the German magazine *Brigitte*, journalists who helped to capture her as an adult on tape, were generous and especially helpful with their transcripts. Barbara Baker of *Time-Life* gave her superb assistance in the selection of photographs, once again, and I want to thank Richard Stolley and Richard Burgheim of *People* for encouraging me to indulge in show business biography week after week.

Beverly Hills   ROBERT WINDELER
July 1975

Introduction

She was, without possibility of argument, the most famous child in the world. The image of her very public childhood belongs to the ages, although she never made a single motion picture that she or anybody else thought was really any good. Starting in films at three years old, Shirley Temple was just playing games, and so, in a sense, were the tens of millions in her audiences. The chief game was called 'Beat the Depression' (a harsh reality never visible in any of Shirley's fantastical films), and more than any other person, she did just that—at least according to Franklin D. Roosevelt, who presided over the United States of America for all the years she was a child star, and who probably did the second most in beating the Depression.

In the 1930s, six year olds of all ages made Shirley Temple box office queen of the world for a record four years running, when she was aged seven to ten (although her parents and the studio lied that she was six to nine). She was *Time*'s 'cinemoppet', and the youngest person ever to appear on the magazine's cover; the youngest person ever listed in *Who's Who*, and the youngest ever to get an Academy Award.

Not only was she a kind of midget folk heroine but an attraction for the world's great who also beat a path to her dressing-room door. Eleanor Roosevelt, Noël Coward, J. Edgar Hoover and Thomas Mann left the soundstages of Twentieth Century-Fox (as all her prominent visitors did) proudly wearing a Shirley Temple Police Force badge. Her official eighth birthday (really her ninth) brought more than 135,000 presents from around the world, including a baby kangaroo from Australia and a prize Jersey calf from a class of schoolchildren in Oregon. In 1938 her income was the seventh highest in America (the top six were industrialists, including MGM's Louis B. Mayer), at $307,014, and that was just before she started earning $300,000 per picture, and making three or four a year.

Others had paved the way for the possibility of a Shirley Temple. Principally, they were Mary Pickford (who, when a woman in her twenties and thirties, played children of ten or twelve in silent features), Jackie Coogan (who had played *The Kid* with Charlie Chaplin in 1920 and appeared in *Peck's Bad Boy* and *Oliver Twist*), and Hal Roach, with his *Our Gang* series beginning in 1921. But they had worked their magic in combinations of drama, melodrama and mayhem in the silents.

Shirley was born in 1928, the year sound films really took over, and she made her first films in 1932, the year Pickford retired. Shirley had a brand new medium in which both more and less were required of a child. There was less acting, certainly, but more singing, dancing, shaking the finger, bowing the mouth to actually say something—like 'oh, my goodness'—and, above all, dimpling. And no one did any of those things better or more appealingly than Shirley.

The child stars who came after her were different too. Mickey Rooney and Judy Garland were really adolescents with other kinds of situations in their films, and Judy's musicals—

albeit escapist—had more lasting merit than Shirley's and were made in Technicolour, something Shirley experienced only briefly. Tiny Margaret O'Brien in the 1940s was more of an actress than Shirley, and at her most brilliant in scary circumstances. World War II brought more serious subject matter to films. As realism overtook fantasy in the movies in the 1950s there was no longer a place for child stars. Brandon de Wilde and Hayley Mills were the two exceptions in the 1950s and 1960s. In 1974 ten-year-old Tatum O'Neal won an Oscar as the con-child in *Paper Moon*. But as Buddy Ebsen, Shirley's dancing partner in the 1936 *Captain January* groused, 'That's no child, that's a hoodlum. Where did they go?'

Where indeed. But while she lasted, little Shirley Temple was an original. As Bill 'Bojangles' Robinson, her most famous dancing partner, put it: 'God made her just all by herself—no series, Just one.' When she got to be a gangly thirteen-year-old Shirley wisely retired from films, to go to school for the first time. She came back with limited success for a series of roles as a teenager, and quit the cinema world for good in 1949. She was twenty-one, just at the age most people start to work for a living, and her self-earned fortune of between three and four million dollars was intact.

At that age she had already survived her young marriage to John Agar, and the divorce from him that had created the only scandal of her life. She was the mother of a one-year-old daughter and ready to try marriage and motherhood all over again. More importantly, she survived the whole of her early life and emerged as a sane and contributing human being. Whatever reservations others may have had about Shirley Temple as an adult, she herself had none.

Jackie Coogan had had to sue his mother and step-father to recover even a small percentage of the four million dollars he earned as a child (thereby inspiring the state of California's 'Coogan Law', which protected Shirley, and those who followed, from grasping guardians). Shirley's father, on the other hand, was a banker who invested her earnings wisely and mostly on her behalf. Other former child stars, unable to cope with growing up or suddenly not being adored by millions, retreated into other pursuits—alcohol, multiple marriages, dope or pills. A few kept trying to get work as actors, since acting was the only thing they knew how to do.

Still others got as far away from Hollywood as fast as they could. English-born Freddie Bartholomew, most famous for the talkie remake of *Little Lord Fauntleroy* and *David Copperfield*, became an advertising executive on New York's Madison Avenue. Canada's Deanna Durbin, after a decade of Hollywood stardom, mostly in musicals, turned her back so firmly on the fame and glamour of her former profession that she refused even to talk about it. In anonymity, she later lived in a small village an hour outside Paris, with her husband and two children. Villagers knew her only as Madame David and acted to protect her privacy. Someone from a garage opposite her farmhouse warned her of unfamiliar visitors, and she never answered the door or telephone herself.

Margaret O'Brien, the biggest child star of the 1940s, earned an Academy Award at eight, $2,500 a week at nine, and top-ten box office ranking in both 1944 and 1945. Although she had to make some severe adjustments to young adulthood, Margaret never regretted her childhood, and continued in an acting career, mostly on television, in the 1960s and 1970s. Dean Stockwell, *The Boy With Green Hair* and a star of *Gentleman's Agreement*, was outspoken in his bitterness. It's a miserable way to bring up a child,' he said. 'The life of a child star frustrates normal interests and associations with other children. I had no friends except my brother and I never did what I wanted to do. I had one vacation in nine years.'

Shirley had none of these problems or adjustments. After her divorce from John Agar and a happy second marriage, to Charles Black, she left Hollywood and found a new life in different places—in Washington D.C., Northern California, New York and Ghana. She raised two more children and returned to her home town only intermittently in the late 1950s and early 1960s for television work, always staying in hotels and leaving the minute work was over. Living down her former self was not a problem for her 'within my circle of friends or really with anyone, except a few middle-aged people who are stuck on this image of the little girl', she said just before going to Africa in 1974 to be United States Ambassador to Ghana. 'That's their problem.'

She made a clear distinction between herself and that screen character of over thirty-five years ago. 'I have always thought of her as 'the little girl'. I never had a sister and she's sort of like that. She's opened up a lot of doors for me because she's known all over the world and that's a big advantage for me. I know her well and I even remember some of the dance routines she did, but she's not me.'

Twenty-five years of volunteer work, local and national Republican politics, work at the United Nations and on problems of the environment, led Mrs Black to prominence in diplomatic circles. Tragedy struck in late 1972, in the form of breast cancer, but Shirley became the first public figure to make her mastectomy public to help those similarly afflicted, and got more than 50,000 letters praising her action. It was only a temporary setback.

In 1975 the scrapbooks of her show business career lined the shelves of the library in her large Tudor home in Woodside, California (a suburb south of San Francisco that someone once called a hotbed of social rest), and prints of her films were in the toolshed. She herself was in Ghana, not only living in the world, but trying hard to make it better.

Chapter One

While hopeful stage mothers and their progeny from all sections of the United States and Canada descended on Hollywood at an estimated rate of 400 a day in the 1930s, ironically, most of the little boys and girls who made it big in movies were native Californians, starting with Los Angeles-born Jackie Coogan. Perhaps this was because they were brought up to be less frenzied about the show side of show business (and more canny about the business side), or simply because they were in exactly the right place at exactly the right time. Whatever the reason, the biggest child star of all was no exception to the rule. Shirley Jane Temple was born at 9 pm, 23 April 1928, at Santa Monica Hospital in Santa Monica, a small city on the Pacific Ocean, but a scant dozen miles west of Hollywood.

'Long before she was born I tried to influence her future life by association with music, art and natural beauty,' her mother, Gertrude Temple, said in 1934. 'Perhaps this prenatal preparation helped make Shirley what she is.' Nothing else in Shirley's background accounted for her career, except that Gertrude herself had wanted to act. But, instead, this daughter of a Chicago jeweller had attended Polytechnic High School in Los Angeles and met and married George Temple when she was only seventeen. Born in Fairview, Pennsylvania, of Pennsylvania Dutch parentage he had arrived in Los Angeles as a child in 1903. Although his family specialised in medicine, he had opted for banking. When Shirley was born the Temples owned a one-storey stucco house in Santa Monica, and a small La Salle sedan. They had two sons, Jack and George Jnr., who were twelve and seven at the time of Shirley's birth.

'My mother was kind of afraid to have a third child,' Shirley recalled, 'because she wanted a girl but she was afraid she would have another boy. So my dad went to the family doctor and he said, "If you have your tonsils out you will have a girl." So they removed my Dad's tonsils and they grew back. He had to have them out a second time, and, nine months after the second operation, I was born. There is no medical reason for this story, but I think it's funny and so I wanted to tell it, even though it always makes my parents angry.'

Shirley walked at thirteen months and, when she was two, according to her mother, 'she began to display a rare sense of rhythm and would keep time with her feet to the music on the radio'. When Shirley was three, Gertrude wanted to enrol her in a professional dancing class for children whose parents entertained screen ambitions for them. George very reluctantly agreed. He was a young banker with three children. This was the Depression and the bank had already closed several times. There had been wholesale paycuts, and fifty cents a week for dance lessons was a lot in 1931. While Shirley quickly became the baby star pupil of her class at Meglin Dancing School, it wasn't the lessons, according to Mrs Temple, that could 'be credited with developing Shirley's personality. That is something she always had.'

Just as stage mothers hounded them, movie talent scouts regularly scoured dancing and singing schools for children, hoping to pick up a prodigy for a modest salary. Charles Lamont, a director at Educational Studios, was on the prowl for precocious tots not more than three feet high. The day he arrived at Shirley's school she was under-dressed for a rainy day. Mrs Temple was apparently the only mama who didn't know of the talent search; the other girls were in their Sunday best. 'I hid under the piano,' Shirley recalled. 'Obviously no poise. He stood around for a while watching and then he said, "I'll take the one under the piano." '

Still two years in age away from kindergarten, which she would never get to, Shirley was signed on at Educational at ten dollars a day to appear in a series of one-reel Baby Burlesks, take-offs on adult movies and stars. She played Lulu Parsnips, a satire on columnist Louella Parsons (who later became one of Shirley's greatest champions), and played a baby in a nappy held by outsized safety pins in *The Pie Covered Wagon*. She even spoke a French phrase—'Oui, mon cher'—to a nappy-clothed boy in a spoof of *What Price Glory? Polly-tix in Washington, Kid 'n' Hollywood* and *Kid 'n' Africa* (a satire of *Trader Horn* and *Tarzan and His Mate*) were typical titles in the Baby Burlesks series of 1933. In the latter, Shirley played Madame Cradlebait, a missionary who ends up in a cannibal's cooking pot. Mrs Black, in her role as U.S. Ambassador to Ghana, could only hope that Ghanaians never got to see this very early film of hers, since it represents a white man's view of black Africa and black Africans in the most stereotyped terms.

Nonetheless, Shirley called the Educational series of one-reelers 'the best things I ever did. I was "The Incomparable More-Legs Sweet Trick", Marlene Deitrich, and wore feathers and an arrow through my head.' She graduated to two-reelers for Educational, *Frolics of Youth*, at fifteen dollars a day. Producer Jack Hays signed her to a contract at fifty dollars per picture, which he tried to hold her to after she left and signed with Twentieth Century-Fox. In court Hays produced a contract giving him exclusive right to Shirley Temple's services, but it was signed only in her childish scrawl and was thrown out by the judge.

Gertrude had hustled Shirley around the studios, enouraged by her success at Educational, and fired with ambition for her daughter. George's position at the bank had improved, so the money was now secondary. Shirley had been rejected along with thousands of others by Hal Roach for the *Our Gang* comedies, and by Fox and most of the other studios. She managed a few small roles in major productions, but thankfully, there were always the *Frolics of Youth* to fall back on. In 1932 Shirley did a bit part for Capitol in her first full-length feature *The Red-Haired Alibi.*

Billed as Shirley Jane Temple she did a small role in a Zane Grey western directed by Henry Hathaway and starring Randolph Scott, *To The Last Man,* for Paramount in 1933. *Out All Night* for Universal the same year gave her the chance to work with one of Mary Pickford's old directors, Sam Taylor, and with Slim Summerville and Zasu Pitts, who predicted greatness for the child. Shirley made a musical with Janet Gaynor, Lionel Barrymore and Robert Young but her part was too small for her to have a song. She also took another bit part in *Mandalay,* a Kay Francis vehicle directed by Michael Curtiz. But no one except Miss Pitts had yet singled her out as anything more remarkable than just another cute kid.

It was one of her *Frolics of Youth,* entitled *Pardon My Puffs* that led to Shirley Temple's real breakthrough. At a Beverly Hills preview of the two-reeler, song-writer Jay Gourney was struck by her work and asked Gertrude to have Shirley audition for his partner Lew Brown for a speciality number at the end of a feature tentatively called *Fox Follies.* After hearing almost two hundred other applicants, Brown (who had also given Jackie Cooper his big movie break) gave Shirley the job the moment she finished singing the song, *Baby Take a Bow*.

With just two weeks of specialised training and rehearsal at the Fox studios Shirley recorded the song. The film, based on an idea by Will Rogers, and centred on a mythical United States Secretary of Amusements who would cheer the country up during the Depression by organising government-sponsored vaudeville acts, was retitled *Stand Up and Cheer*. Shirley wore a white dress with red polka dots, duplicates of which would later be marketed in her name, for her number with James Dunn. It was the very last in the film, and she quite simply stole the picture, even causing most reviewers, who had dozed off, to revive.

Even before the release of *Stand Up and Cheer*, Winfield Sheehan, Fox's vice-president in charge of production, who, along with everyone else who had witnessed her 'début' during filming, was captivated by Shirley's talent, tied her up with a seven-year contract at $150 weekly. Before she was six, and even at this relatively modest salary for movies, Shirley was already out-earning her father. Although Shirley was actually six in April of 1934, the Temples and the studio conspired to subtract a year from her age, possibly to prolong her kiddy career and make her seem even more precocious than she was. All official biographical material on Shirley was issued with 23 April 1929, as her birthdate, and it was only when she was 'twelve', actually thirteen, that Shirley herself found out—along with the rest of the world—how old she really was.

Both the song *Baby Takes A Bow*, and the Movie, *Stand Up and Cheer* were hits on release in early 1934, and she was the only thing novel about the picture. Newspapers ran still photographs of Shirley from the film in preference to those of the stars, who included Warner Baxter and Madge Evans. Exhibitors began billing the film 'Shirley Temple in *Stand Up and Cheer*' even though the studio's official credits had her way down the list, lumped with others in the speciality numbers category. The fan mail for her began to come in at a relative trickle, twenty or thirty letters a day. Then it jumped to two hundred, then five hundred.

Shirley was clearly a star, but Hollywood still distrusted its children. Other actors didn't like to play with them; some grown-ups wouldn't pay to see them; they were a nuisance on the set, temperamental and hard to teach. Fox, not quite knowing how to deal with her, let Shirley go to Paramount on 'loan' for two films. In the first, *Little Miss Marker*, she played the memorable title role in Damon Runyan's story, the orphan who reforms bookie Sorrowful Jones, (Adolphe Menjou, who was equally memorable). 'No more engaging child has been beheld on the screen,' wrote the *New York Times* critic Mordaunt Hall on the release of *Little Miss Marker*, in May 1934.

Until she saw herself on the screen for the first time in *Little Miss Marker*, Shirley had seen only one movie, *Skippy*, starring Jackie Cooper. She liked herself in the Paramount film, and applauded often during the preview. The reviews of *Little Miss Marker* were read to her, but the fan mail most carefully was not, since almost all of it said things like 'I think you are the most beautiful baby in the world.'

After her second film at Paramount, *Now and Forever* with Carole Lombard and Gary Cooper, Shirley returned to Fox for minor roles in *Now I'll Tell*, with Spencer Tracy, Helen Twelvetrees and Alice Faye, and *Change of Heart*, a Janet Gaynor-Charles Farrell vehicle. Spurred on by the million-dollar gross their rival studio had reaped on *Little Miss Marker*, Fox now made *Baby Take a Bow*, borrowing the song title and giving Shirley star billing, but below the title.

'I was really a fortunate person to be in movies at that time,' Shirley remembered in 1974. 'I had a lot of fun, caused a lot of trouble. I was a tomboy, although no one really knew that because they always saw me in the nice little dresses, and gloves. I really wanted to be a G-woman ... or a vegetable salesman, or a pie salesman. Then when I became a teenager I got a little more class and decided I wanted to be a brain surgeon, but I figured no one would come to me. I never really wanted to be an actress. I just enjoyed all of this because when you start anything at age three, you don't realise it is work.'

Gertrude, while dedicated to Shirley's career, was more unassuming and less pushy than most of her fellow stage mothers. 'I had a very shy mother, and she is still a very shy mother,' Shirley said shortly before Gertrude and George celebrated their sixtieth wedding anniversary at the end of 1974. 'My mother made all of our clothes and was a real homemaker. I think she first sent me to dancing school to get me out of the house. She was the only one who ever spanked me and she only spanked me once. I was very firm-skinned— and still am—and I broke the ruler she used on the first swat.'

Mrs Temple had been concerned that in *Little Miss Marker* Shirley had hung out with gangsters and said things like 'Aw nuts'. She was assured that after *Baby Takes A Bow* Shirley's screenplays would be 'more suitable to her cheery personality'. And for the rest of the 1930s they were tailormade to Miss Temple's image, if not to Miss Temple. Father George continued to oversee the family finances—including Shirley's. 'I never cared about money when I was little,' Shirley said.

George Temple was short, very stocky, with protruding pot and posterior, thinning dark hair and brown eyes, a snub nose and the dimples of his daughter. He invariably dressed in a grey suit off the peg. His wife was good-looking, taller than he, with olive skin, high cheekbones and an affable large mouth that spoke in a rather flat voice. Her regular, slightly hard features were well-preserved, and she took good care of herself and her face. She looked nothing like Shirley, which led to outrageous propositions to George from women who wanted a daughter like Shirley. 'My parents didn't smoke or drink,' said Shirley, 'and never went to Hollywood parties.'

By the summer of 1934 six-year-old Shirley Temple was established as a full-fledged movie star. Her contract with the newly amalgamated Twentieth Century-Fox was adjusted—mostly at the instigation of her banker father—and her weekly salary leapt from $150 to $1,000. In addition, the new agreement provided a clutch of dolls and a Shetland pony for Shirley, as well as 'comfortable and exclusive dressing room facilities', and a $250 weekly salary for Mrs Gertrude Temple. The contract, at Mama's insistence, called for Shirley to be barred from the studio's commissary to prevent her being 'petted and pampered'.

A ten-room bungalow belonging to Lilian Harvey was converted from an exotic contraption to a kiddy-cozy set-side home for Shirley. But for a few weeks she had to violate her new contract by eating at the Fox commissary because she couldn't get into her bungalow until Gloria Swanson, in temporary residence, moved out. There was also a clause in the new Temple contract to the effect that, if Shirley's parents felt her screen work was changing her personality or keeping her from a normal girlhood, they could break the contract and retire their daughter. 'We'd do so, too,' Mrs Temple assured the press.

With her sons away at school, Jack at Stanford and George Jnr. at New Mexico Military Institute, Gertrude was able to devote all her time to Shirley, and she never left the child's side at work, and seldom after hours. Officially, Gertrude was paid her Fox salary (later raised to $500 a week) to manage, dress and chaperone Shirley, and certainly to keep the golden curls in order. Unofficially, Mother Temple was the go-between for director and child star, and she was expected to keep Shirley unspoiled and from getting too far ahead in her education. By strictly forbidding advanced books and most outside influences, Shirley's parents held her back to the point that, when she took a Pitner-Cunningham I.Q. test at the University of California at Los Angeles, Shirley, aged seven years three months, tested only at nine years, seven months, despite an obvious and demonstrated precocity that everyone expected would merit an eleven-year-old's rating.

With regular work—she made no fewer than eight movies in 1934—Shirley's life began to take on a regular rhythm. She woke each morning at seven, was given a glass of orange juice and then lay in bed for forty-five minutes, going over her lines and rehearsing dance steps lying on her back and waving her little legs in the air. After a breakfast of stewed fruit (her favourite was canned pears), one soft boiled egg from the bantam chickens she kept at the studio, and bacon or cereal on alternate mornings, she and her mother went to the studio in their modest La Salle, arriving at 9 am for school even on mornings when there was no Temple film shooting.

Shirley had a standard school desk in her bungalow and used California-issued textbooks, returning them to the state at the end of the year. Miss Frances Klampt ('Klammie'), under the supervision of the Los Angeles Board of Education, taught Shirley the regular school curriculum (complete with yearly examinations) and also served as a social service worker, overseeing Shirley's daily working conditions. During the filming of a picture, Shirley took her lessons in the half-hour change of camera and lighting set-ups between scenes in the morning and took three hours for lessons in the afternoon.

Her lunch hour was just exactly that, in her bungalow, and she ate her biggest meal of the day, although supper at home at six was a hefty soup, salad, three vegetables, a small amount of meat and a light pudding. After playing with her father and rehearsing her lines and routines for the next day with her mother, Shirley went to bed. Her friends were carefully selected from among her neighbours and contemporaries and their parents were requested not to take the children to Shirley's movies lest they get the idea that she was something special. However, her stand-in at the studio was Mary Lou Islieb, a neighbour and the daughter of a branch bank manager who had worked with Mr Temple.

At the studio Shirley was maternal toward her bantam chickens, a dozen rabbits, and dolls from all over the world dressed in native costume. And while she was not prone to cry when she hurt herself, she burst into an almost hysterical fit of sobbing when her favourite doll's arm fell off. She, in turn, was tractable to direction and instinctively obedient to the wishes of adults. The usually well-behaved, obsessively cheerful and optimistic Shirley Temple that her hordes of adoring fans saw on screen was the Shirley Temple behind the scenes as well, bright and lively, with a personality stopping just short of sass. A friend introduced H. G. Wells to Shirley on the set, saying, 'He is the most important man in the Universe.' Shirley contradicted with, 'Oh, no, the most important one is God and Governor Merriam is second.'

Bright Eyes, Shirley's last movie in 1934, and the first in a long string of Shirley Temple Christmas—and Easter—pictures, was a landmark film for her in many ways. Her billing was raised to above the title

SHIRLEY TEMPLE

in

BRIGHT EYES

In the movie she sang what is probably the closest thing she had to a theme song : *On The Good Ship Lollipop*. *Bright Eyes*, in which Shirley again played an orphan—this time 'uncled' by flier Jimmy Dunn, who was forced to parachute out of his plane with Shirley held tight in his arms—also introduced Jane Withers to leading roles as everybody's favourite brat and the perfect foil for Shirley's goodness, as Jane on film was wild, mischievous, noisy and messy.

Bright Eyes also made financial history for Fox. It cost $190,000 to produce and regained its cost in just three weeks of first-run engagements. Shirley's fan mail soared to 2,500 letters per week. *Bright Eyes* and her seven other films in 1934 put Shirley in eighth place in the *Motion Picture Herald*'s box office poll of exhibitors for the year, behind Will Rogers, Clark Gable, Janet Gaynor, Wallace Beery, Mae West, Joan Crawford and Bing Crosby. In 1935, 1936, 1937 and 1938 Shirley topped the *Motion Picture Herald* poll, the only star ever to do it four years in a row. The studio insured her for $25,000 with Lloyds of London—because United States companies refused, on the grounds of age. Lloyds did insist, as a condition of the insurance, that Shirley should not take up arms in warfare or join the army in peacetime; the insurance would be voided if the six year old died or was injured while intoxicated.

In February 1935, at the annual banquet of the Academy of Motion Picture Arts and Sciences, Shirley was awarded an honorary gold statuette for 1934 for having 'achieved eminence among the greatest of screen actors'. The citation that went with her Oscar read 'there was one great towering figure in the cinema game in 1934, one artiste among artists, one giant among troupers. The award is bestowed because Shirley Temple brought more happiness to millions of children and millions of grown-ups than any child of her years in the history of the world.' Even at that time Shirley had some perspective on the situation, and she put the Oscar with her other dolls. And in later years she was the first to admit that acting had nothing to do with it.

Chapter Two

'What are we going to pretend today?' little Shirley would ask her mother and the director, in that order. 'She didn't act or make pictures,' said David Butler, the director of *Bright Eyes*, *The Little Colonel*, *The Littlest Rebel* and *Captain January*. 'She played wonderful games. She got into fairyland, she believed it all herself and that's why you believed it.'

At first Shirley tended to confuse her scripts with reality. During the filming of *Our Little Girl* early in 1935 she had to say to Lyle Talbot in one scene, 'And anyway I don't like you.' As soon as the scene was shot Shirley went over to Talbot and said solemnly, 'I'm sorry, Mr Talbot, but those lines are in the script; I really do like you.'

But with each picture her camera technique improved. The simple scenes were pure play, no more tiring than dressing her dolls and not so exhausting as a game of hide-and-seek. And if a director about to shoot an over-the-shoulder close-up said, 'Now, Shirley . . .' she would get annoyed with herself and interrupt him with 'You want me to be here, don't you?' and move so that her head was in full frame instead of slightly blocked by the other actor's chin or cheek.

Shirley always knew when she had made a mistake in the middle of a difficult scene or a complicated dance routine and would hold up her little hand to spoil the take so that a new one would have to be started, pre-empting, like many later actresses, the director's prerogative to yell 'cut'. She wasn't overly sensitive to criticism. 'You can do lots better than that,' director Butler told her after a scene in *Captain January*. Shirley winked, as she had seen her older colleagues do and admitted, 'There was a little faking in it.'

In singing silently to her own playback, moving her lips while a recording machine played a record already prepared by her of the tune she was singing for the camera, she achieved an uncanny perfection and always looked as if she were singing the tune on screen. Her lips were never out of 'sync'. Incredibly, she did many times what few other singers on the screen have done once—made a perfectly synchronised playback in the first take.

Her association with the sharper show business men and women she met at work, most of whom took a special interest in her, gave Shirley at ages six, seven and eight the professionalism, easy repartee and love of catch phrases of a seasoned trouper. She whooped with delight when her mentor and favourite dancing partner, Bill (Bojangles) Robinson told her the vaudeville wheeze "How's the tailoring business?—So-so."

When she sat down to play her favourite game of squares she'd often say, "There aren't any spots on your suit but you're going to the cleaners." Her precocity annoyed Dr Oscar Olson, president of the Senate of Sweden when she beat him at squares (connecting dots with lines to form the most boxes) twice in succession. Shirley's other set-side games included cribbage, which she learned at five years old, draughts, parchesi and casino. She was at home with the studio wits, the fun-lovers and avoided anyone who seemed moody or preoccupied.

For this reason her least favourite director was Irving Cummings (*Curly Top, The Poor Little Rich Girl*), a nervous, temperamental man who screamed if there was any noise on the set : 'Give me a break—you see what I'm up against here, don't you? I've got a baby here, I'm working with a kid." Shirley was hurt and bewildered. Wasn't it okay to be a kid? She played scenes mechanically and didn't laugh much in the Cummings pictures, but when she changed directors again the legendary effervescent giggle came back.

On any set Shirley never quite seemed to be paying attention. When her mother, the director, or any other player coached her, she would look down at her feet and roll her eyes around the room like any distracted youngster, and even bounce a ball or play jacks. But learning routines had started so early for her that she got them the first time, while seeming to be doing something else. Her coaches seldom had to repeat instructions. In a single morning, less time than it took with adults, Bill Robinson taught her a soft-shoe number, a waltz clog and three tap-dance routines. Shirley never looked at him once during this session but learned all the numbers from listening to his feet.

Robinson, her idol and co-star in 1935's *The Little Colonel* and *The Littlest Rebel*, said she was the greatest tap dancer for her age then living, and he swore he would make her the greatest in the world someday. She called him 'Uncle Billy'. He taught Shirley strenuous routines without letting her know it was work or allowing her to become tired.

'That was very copacetic, Shirley,' he would say, 'now we'll try it once more.'

Or, 'How'd you like to sit right down on that bench and watch your Uncle Bill do the routine? Then maybe he'll connect you with a nice Coca-cola.'

Or, 'Bet you a nickel you can't do it again—who's gwine to be the judge?'

Jack Donahue, the choreographer of *Curly Top* and *Captain January*, was rehearsing a song called *You Take Two Steps and Truck on Down* with Shirley and he asked Robinson, 'What am I going to do then?'

'Why you truck on down,' came the reply.

'Can she truck?' asked Donahue.

'Sure she can,' replied Robinson.

When the scene was over Robinson got Shirley into a corner and asked, 'Why didn't you tell Jack you could truck?'

'Don't be funny,' she answered. 'I'm not giving away any of our steps!'

During another Robinson-Temple routine some dancers from a neighbouring production company came on to the set to watch them. Bill gave the signal to the pianist and said, 'Come on, Shirley, let's do it.' She shook her head no, uncharacteristically. Robinson took her aside and asked what was the matter. 'If we do it now they'll steal it,' she said. 'We'll only do it when they're ready to shoot.'

'I didn't have to look at Bill Robinson's feet when he was teaching me to dance,' she remembered. 'We had our mental symphony together and he was a marvellous teacher and I still remember some of his dances. He was the greatest.'

Another of Shirley's idols was Will Rogers, with whom she never had the chance to make a movie. (He was killed in a plane crash in 1935). But he taught her to ride and she often visited him at his ranch. She so admired the cowboy that, after his death, she would not let anyone sing or whistle his favourite song, *The Last Roundup*, in her presence.

But throughout the next few years, Shirley's mother remained her most important coach. 'Sparkle, Shirley, sparkle,' she would call to her daughter at various times during filming. If Shirley had to cry in a scene her mother would take her outside and give her a stern talking to for several minutes. Back in front of the camera, Shirley cried without effort. 'It's in the script,' she said whenever she was asked if she minded crying on cue. Gertrude taught Shirley her parts by reading them aloud several times over, after supper. Because this aural method of learning lines made it necessary to learn all the other parts in a script, Shirley often astonished her co-workers by correcting them when they muffed their dialogue.

'Mrs Temple is much more Shirley's director than I am,' said Irving Cummings. 'She teaches her her lines, coaches her on how to say them, suggests Shirley's expressions, shows her how to stand and sit and walk and talk and run. There's really very little left for a director to do when Shirley arrives on the scene.'

Shirley wasn't critical of her own performances but what did interest her was seeing what scenes had been cut from the final prints of her movies; she was disappointed if one of her favourites was left out. Her only other serious complaint in her first two years at the Fox studios was that her bungalow didn't have a swing. The property department put one up on the tree next to her dressing room but, when a studio mogul saw her swinging high over Janet Gaynor's bungalow next door, he ordered the swing removed. He didn't want the lot's biggest box-office draw to fall and hurt herself.

In March 1935, Shirley was asked to put her foot and handprints in the forecourt of Grauman's Chinese Theatre in Hollywood, and she wrote in her childish scrawl her message to the world: 'Love to You all.' In April, her birthday party was postponed from the 23rd because she had the sniffles. 'When Shirley sniffles, it costs us $5,000,' said Bud DeSylva, the producer of *The Little Colonel*, Shirley's first film of that year.

The Little Colonel was based on Annie Fellow Johnston's Southern story, and it had Shirley reuniting her mother with her estranged grandfather, played by Lionel Barrymore, and following Bojangles Robinson in his famous stair dance. When

*Even when eighteen months old, Shirley
(called 'Presh' by her mother) knew how
to flash her dimples, 1929.*

(Above left)
*The two-reel **Burlesks** were heavily costumed and usually bitingly on target.*

(Above)
*Her first — and in her view, her best — films were **Baby Burlesks** in which Shirley and other three and four year olds spoofed well known people and situations, 1932-33.*

Before Fred Astaire and Ginger Rogers, Bill
('Bojangles') Robinson and Shirley Temple
were the 1930s' favourite dance team.

(Above top)
Shirley always liked uniforms and
costumes, but sometimes her
cowboy boots pinched.

Shirley liked to be involved in some
of the peripheral movie-making
jobs; here she helps to unload
caterer's lunches on out-of-town
location, 1934.

Mama Gertrude Temple always knew
best, and coached and guided Shirley
in her childhood career.

*The Angel-face that won hundreds of
millions of film-goers' hearts worldwide,
1935.*

*With her mother and father Shirley took
an Hawaiian vacation in 1936, to the
delight of her fans in the islands, and it
became the first of many.*

she and Robinson finished rehearsing the staircase dance in *The Little Colonel*, he knelt down crying tears of joy, and kissed each of her tiny dancing feet. 'God, he made her just all by herself,' said 'Uncle Bill'. 'No series. Just one. Uncle Bill doesn't tell her feet where to go, her heart tells her.'

She did three more films in 1935, half the previous year's output, but she was starring in all of them. *Our Little Girl* with Joel McCrea and *Curly Top*, in which she introduced *Animal Crackers in My Soup* and *When I Grow Up*, further established her as the biggest motion picture box-office draw of the mid-1930s. And in *The Littlest Rebel*, another Civil War story, Shirley dances on the sidewalk with Bill Robinson to raise money for a trip North to Washington, where, in hoopskirt and ruffles, she pleads with Abraham Lincoln for the release of her father (John Boles), who has been captured by the Union while visiting his dying wife. Her sobbing pleas are interrupted frequently to eat slices of apple that President Lincoln has been peeling.

Shirley Temple pictures had many distinguished co-stars, but she really didn't need their support to sell her vehicles. That was a good thing since most established actors are reluctant to work with a child anyway, since children invariably stole scenes. Lionel Barrymore had been adamant in refusing to play with Shirley, but after *The Little Colonel* was completed the aging actor, living alone at the time, and badly crippled with arthritis, said 'I feel like a happier man.' He began to cry when Shirley asked him to sign her autograph book.

Gloria Stuart didn't want to appear with Shirley and was furious about the favouritism shown Shirley in camera angles on the remake of *Rebecca of Sunnybrook Farm*. Alice Faye, the veteran of two Temple properties (*Poor Little Rich Girl* and *Stowaway*) said to Gloria, 'Why worry? Temple will steal the picture anyway.' And Adolphe Menjou, her co-star in

Paramount's highly successful *Little Miss Marker*, had said, 'That Temple kid scares me. She knows all the tricks. She backs me out of the camera, blankets me, crabs my laughs. She's making a stooge of me. Well, she's an Ethel Barrymore at four.'

In real life Shirley was given an allowance of $4.25 weekly, while the rest of her $1,000 salary was carefully invested by her father in gilt-edged securities, annuities and selected bonds, all picked with mid-Depression wariness. From the $4.25 Shirley put $1.50 in her toy bank and in a typical week in 1935 spent: on candy, 25 cents, fruit, 40 cents, soda pop, 15 cents, a box of paints, 75 cents, dog collar, 95 cents, and Sunday School collection, 25 cents.

In the fantasy world her movies were now making from $1 million to $1.5 million on their first releases alone—and this at a time when most of the audience, children, paid only 15 cents to get into the cinema. Temple routinely packed 2,000-seat houses in big cities for afternoon performances and did only slightly less well at night. Her pictures did even better on second and third runs. What made her box-office appeal even more extraordinary was the fact that her pictures were cheap to make, costing usually between $200,000-300,000. They had simple stories, few sets, mostly indoor, and small shooting companies. They were often brought in a week or ten days under their estimated shooting schedule.

By the end of 1935 Shirley had 'X'-ed, and her parents had signed, a revised contract with Twentieth Century-Fox: $4,000 a week over all fifty-two weeks of the calendar year, a bonus of more than $20,000 per picture plus $500 a week for Gertrude. Under product tie-in deals with ten firms for Shirley Temple dolls, and underwear, coats, hats, shoes, books, hair ribbons, soap, dresses, toys, cereal bowls and milk pitchers she received another $1,000 a week, and her mother an additional $100 a week.

Besides being the most important screen actress, Shirley Temple had quickly become the most important singer on screen. By introducing a song in a movie she automatically made it a hit, and top song writers of the day such as Harry Warren, Irving Caesar, Paul Francis Webster, Richard Whiting and Mack Gordon turned out material for Shirley. Sheet music for her *Polly Wolly Doodle* and *The Good Ship Lollipop* ran over 400,000 copies each, topping the sales of any song introduced in the same period by Bing Crosby, Nelson Eddy, Alice Faye or any other movie singer. Her 1935 Shirley Temple Christmas song-book sold 250,000 copies. And her popularity was world-wide as well. In Japan, where she was also the top box-office star, a thirty-six-page book of pictures of Shirley, with no text in any language, sold over 1,200,000 copies.

The lives of George and Gertrude Temple were drastically altered by their daughter's accession to the top ranks of movie stars. At the beginning of 1934 George had been just a bank teller at the California Bank branch at 16th and Vermont in Los Angeles. He was quickly promoted to branch manager after his bank showed a marked increase in children's savings accounts. Just before Shirley's eighth birthday, in April 1936, George was promoted to manager of the larger branch of the California Bank at Hollywood and Cahuenga Boulevards in Hollywood. He moved his family from their modest six-room frame house in Santa Monica to a larger house in a Brentwood canyon, banked on a hillside, and protected on two sides by canyon walls to give the dimpled star privacy from the hordes of enthusiastic fans whose curiosity knew no hours.

The old La Salle was traded in for a long black Cadillac, and now Shirley was always accompanied on the lot and in public by her chauffeur-bodyguard, John Griffith. Griffith was six-foot two, weighed two hundred pounds and had been given the job by Darryl Zanuck whom he had saved from drowning when both were boys in Nebraska. Zanuck had arrived at Fox in 1935 just in time to produce *The Littlest Rebel*, when Shirley's legs started to grow long. Zanuck told his Fox underlings to keep her doll-like dresses short and to have her co-stars lift her up a lot to preserve the illusion of her little-girl lightness.

Despite his size and strength, Shirley had succeeded in hospitalising 'Griff' for two days in Palm Springs. He had chased her for miles through the resort, burdened with his hardware and heavy clothes in the hot sun, while she, having just learned to ride a bicycle, got away from him and escaped down a dusty street. Griff's wife later became Mrs Temple's personal maid.

George, Gertrude and Shirley attempted to take a normal family vacation in the summer of 1935 and sailed off to Hawaii for twelve weeks. But her adoring fans saw them off and greeted their return home. In Honolulu, in near-riot conditions, Shirley was made a member of the Safety Patrol of the Hawaiian resort and presented by the Japanese colony in the territory with what they termed 'The finest and most elaborate bridal doll ever to reach Hawaii; its value is beyond dollars and cents.' It was twice as tall as Shirley.

Neither of Shirley's brothers, Jack and George Jnr (Sonny) had a spark of interest or ambition in show business, although Jack was given a job for a few months in the Fox publicity department, with no qualifications other than being Shirley's brother. He begged to be allowed to go to Stanford instead and no one refused him, although at college his fellow students elected him manager of the Stanford Dramatic Club hoping that something of his little sister had rubbed off on him.

It was Gertrude whose life had truly changed, however. She kept insisting that 'if the day ever comes when I feel that Shirley is becoming self-conscious or too aware of her screen importance I shall cancel her contract immediately and let her grow up to a normal girlhood, far from Hollywood and its studios.' But in the meantime, not only did she have to take care of the child who was suddenly the most beloved and photographed human being in the world, Gertrude felt compelled to tell how she did it in a flood of articles for women's magazines. 'I do not let Shirley get the idea that she is too important in our scheme of existence,' she wrote. 'At home she feels everything revolves around her father.'

Shirley was disciplined when necessary and Gertrude even felt that it would be a good idea for her daughter to get a public spanking in a film, as an example to children and their parents, but the studio wouldn't hear of it. Personal appearances by Shirley, which could have earned her a lot of additional money, were vetoed by George and Gertrude because the public's adulation would be direct and possibly harmful. 'The mother of a famous star has a difficult road to travel,' concluded Gertrude Temple. 'No mother can know how difficult until she has a small celebrity in her own home.'

Chapter Three

In the middle and late 1930s there was only one child star who came even close to rivalling Shirley Temple's enormous popularity: Jane Withers, who couldn't have been more opposite to Shirley's on-screen goody-two-shoes image. Jane was as plain as Shirley was pretty; her straight dark hair was in Dutch-boy bangs while Shirley's golden curls were the envy of half the world's mothers, if not their daughters. 'I was never pretty,' Jane noted, 'thank God, or I'd never have got anything.' But most important, Jane was the hateful hellion to Shirley's lovable angel. Jane yelled and screamed, kicked and bit, deceived and connived her way through twenty-seven starring films in six short years, many with giveaway titles: *The Holy Terror*, *Wild and Woolly*, *Always in Trouble* and *Rascals*.

Her favourite story line, as she described it when aged ten in 1936, was: 'My father's a millionaire, my mother's a great society mother. She takes me to these bridge parties and I throw mud over everybody. I'm just terrible. I'm never good for one minute all through the picture. That is my idea of a swell story; it gives you a chance to yell your head off. Garbo and Dietrich never yell at all. That's the trouble with being a glamour girl—no yelling.' She understood even at that age, however, that her actual scripts could never be that perfect. 'At the end, of course, just to satisfy everybody I get a spanking,' she explained. 'The minute they slapped me in *Bright Eyes*, audiences just yelled and waved they were so happy. I don't mind; I had my fun, so let them have their fun too.'

While every other studio in Hollywood had been looking for another Shirley Temple, the world's model daughter, Twentieth Century-Fox, who had the real thing under contract, had been looking for an antidote, a bratty foil to Shirley's orphan sweetness in the 1935 *Bright Eyes*. Director David Butler interviewed dozens of girls but it was eight-year-old Jane Withers who won him over and won the part with her imitations of Garbo, W. C. Fields *and* a machine gun. In the film, Shirley as a maid's daughter reluctantly adopted by her nouveau riche employers after the mother's death, asks Santa Claus for—what else?—a doll. Jane, the real daughter of the household, became a star when she expressed her disappointment at not receiving a machine gun from Santa by going once again into the body-shaking rat-tat-tat of her audition for Butler. From this supporting part she went straight into starring roles in her own vehicles for Fox with her own production company, and into a secure position as the number two child in the world.

Jane Withers is better known to a couple of generations since the 1930s as Josephine the Plumber in the longest running series of North American television commercials ever filmed. In twenty one-minute segments a year, for more than thirteen years so far, Jane Withers extolled the virtues of Comet Cleanser and its effect on stained sinks—and made more money than she had earned as a top child star in the 1930s. Playing Josephine part-time for so long also opened the way, in 1974, for Jane to make a full-time return to the show business career she had mostly suspended twenty-six years before to marry (twice) and become a mother (five times) and grandmother (once).

Singing, dancing and acting—despite her years away from it came back as naturally as it had come to her the first time, as an infant. The daughter of Atlanta Presbyterians, Lavinia Ruth Elble and Walter Withers, Jane was predestined for an entertainment career even before she was born that rainy night in Georgia, 12 April 1926 (to which fact she attributed being a night person who loved the rain). 'Mother was determined that she was going to have only one child and that it would be a girl and that she would go into show business,' Jane recalled when aged forty-nine. 'She turned down several marriage proposals because the men wouldn't go along with it. When she was carrying me she'd study movie marquees trying to decide on a name to go with Withers. She wanted so much to be in show business herself. She taught me to sing, although she doesn't sing on pitch. Luckily I do, although I never know what key I'm singing in. She'd take me to the movies when I was two and three so I could learn.'

The name Jane fitted the marquees in Lavinia's fantasy world, and the child herself seemed to be co-operating, starting to hum recognisable melodies at seven months of age. Jane danced before she walked, sang before she talked, started studying tap, ballet and character dancing at two years old. (Lavinia's parents had refused her even dancing lessons.) At three years old, Jane sang *Little Pal* at a local amateur night, and learned to do her comic impersonations of Fields, Garbo, Zasu Pitts, and others. 'Fifi D'Orsay was the most fun to do because of the French accent,' the grown-up Jane recalled. Before she was four Jane Withers was a star of *Aunt Sally's Kiddie Review* and then of her own show on WSGT radio in Atlanta. She became the mascot of Georgia Tech and was billed as 'Dixie's Dainty Dewdrop'.

In 1932, having gone as far as she could go in the South, Jane and her mother joined the hordes heading West to Hollywood and the movies. An indulgent husband and father, a modestly-salaried local manager for a tyre and rubber distributor, gave them six months to make it or come home, and a hundred dollars a month to help support them. Ignoring their promise to Daddy, who still sent the stake, for two years Jane and Lavinia lived in boarding houses and trudged around to the studios by streetcar, trying to break on to the big screen. They toted scrapbooks full of the triumphs of Dixie's Dainty Dewdrop on her native soil, but those who hired children for the movies 'couldn't have cared less', so Jane recalled.

She and her mother survived on the extra work Jane was often able to land as one of a cluster of kids 'in over 100 films, a half, three-quarters of a day, workin', waitin', prayin', hopin'.' She got five and seven-and-a-half dollars for one-day calls, and her father spent lunch-hours at the neighbourhood cinema back in Atlanta looking for a glimpse of Janie's uniquely coiffed head. Jane worked on losing her thick Georgia drawl and the Withers women lived on grilled cheese on a hot dog roll with one strip of bacon—eleven cents each—and tuna-fish sandwiches. More than forty years later Jane Withers still loved grilled cheese and bacon and associated it with happy times in Hollywood. From the age of six Janie Withers stood outside the Hollywood Brown Derby with her autograph book in hand, waiting for her favourite adult stars to finish dinner. People in Hollywood were nice to her then, and were ever after.

After the release of *Bright Eyes* established her and her character as everybody's favourite brat—and much closer to a real-life American child of the time than Shirley, certainly—Jane jumped to a Twentieth Century-Fox contract salary of $150 a week. In 1936 she showed up as number thirty-four in box-office appeal when Shirley was in her second year as number one. The studio was forced to raise Jane to $1,500 a week, and give Mrs Withers a consultant's salary of $150 weekly. Fox also had to let the Witherses lend Jane's name to product endorsements *à la* Shirley, a right the studio had been withholding. In 1937 Jane leapt to number six in box-office appeal, and the next year she held on to eighth place. Her salary rose to $2,500 per week. Mrs Withers made careful investments that made Jane independently wealthy in her teens.

Ginger, her first starring role, in 1935, and in many ways her personal favourite, was proto-typical for the nine-year-old tomboy who loved nothing more than a good tussle. As Ginger, she was the orphan daughter of two actors, raised by an old alcoholic ex-Shakespearean player. He gets jailed after a brawl and Jane is taken on by a dotty society dowager who tries to reform the orphan. Jane, within this plot structure, got to do her Garbo and Pitts imitations, a balcony scene from *Romeo and Juliet* and make fresh remarks to her elders like 'skip it' and 'for crying out loud'.

Jane's characters, nonetheless, often did great good in their stories, in many of the same ways as Shirley's did. Jane who, like Shirley and Mary Pickford before them both, frequently played orphans. In *45 Fathers* she saved her wealthy patron from marrying a gold-digger; in *Paddy O'Day*, she reunited lovers; in *Always in Trouble*, she reformed smugglers. By appalling her elders she sometimes transformed them—as she did with Irvin S. Cobb in *Pepper*, changing him from a curmudgeonly miser to a likeable old millionaire. Cobb was won over behind the scenes as well. 'If Jane Withers is a sample of what a movie career does for children, a law should be passed forcing all youngsters to have such an experience,' he said. 'I have yet to know a sweeter, more well-bred, gently considerate and wholly natural little girl.'

Journalists and some segments of the public tried to create

a feud between Jane and Shirley. While they had their unique childhoods and basic niceness—Jane's offscreen only—and tomboyishness—Shirley's offscreen only—in common, the two girls never became friends or even playmates, but they refused throughout their lives to become real-life rivals. Still, while they made only the one film together, filmgoers in later years often mistakenly lumped them together as an antagonistic pair who had made a series of films together.

There could be, and can be, no doubt that Shirley was the top child star and Jane a distinct second fiddle. If the plots of Jane's movies often sounded like Shirley's, it was because they were often Shirley's rejects. Shirley got 5,000 dolls from around the world, Jane only 1,500. Shirley was an honorary colonel in the American Legion and mascot of the Chilean Navy, while Jane had to be content with being 'the world's only honorary chief air hostette of American Airlines', and in continuing to cheer the engineers of Georgia Tech on to football victory as their mascot. First Lady Eleanor Roosevelt joined Shirley Temple's police force after a visit to the studio, while Jane was stuck with sipping soda pop with Teddy Roosevelt's grand-daughter, Pauline Longworth. Shirley's pictures, while never big budget, were 'A' movies, with the studio's best production facilities and co-stars. All of Jane's forty-seven movies as a girl and teenager—except one, Samuel Goldwyn's *North Star*—were even lower budget 'Bs'. Incidentally, Jane made one film as an adult, playing Vashti Snythe in *Giant* at the specific request of director George Stevens.

Lavinia Withers taught her daughter to sew and cook and to budget her allowance of $4.25 a week. She also taught Jane the concept of family councils on major decisions and on spending money. 'I am training Jane to be a poor man's wife,' Mrs Withers asserted. 'I want her to know all the things a girl who marries a man making a modest salary, say forty dollars a week, should and must know.' It turned out Jane didn't need that knowledge for a while. Jane didn't retire when Shirley did—for the first time—in 1940, and, since she had always been a little awkward and podgy anyway, the transition into adolescence wasn't the on-screen trauma for Jane that it was for Shirley. Her comedy got her through Booth Tarkington-type characters such as *Gentle Julia*, and through *Small Town Deb*, her own story—for which she got an extra $3,000 and screen credit as Jerrie Walters.

In *The Girl From Avenue A* Jane wore her first long stockings, and in *Boy Friend* she got her first kiss on the cheek. *Golden Hoofs*, a racetrack film, gave her a handsome leading man from another era, Buddy Rogers, and *A Very Young Lady* gave her two from her own, John Sutton and Richard Clayton, and twenty-seven changes of costume, just like a grown-up leading lady. On loan to Columbia she made *Her First Beau*, co-starring one of the most famous boy child stars then growing up, Jackie Cooper. After her forty-seventh film, *Danger Street* on 20 September 1947, Jane Withers married her first husband, William Moss Jnr, a sometime movie producer and Texas oil millionaire.

Jane quit her lifelong business and moved with Bill first to Midland and Odessa, Texas, then to a ranch he had inherited in New Mexico. The Mosses had three children, Wendy, born in 1948, Bill in 1950, and Randy in 1952, but there was constant friction between themselves. After several years of trying in vain to make the marriage work, the gregarious, fast-moving and bombastic Bill and the deeply religious homebody Jane called it off for ever in 1954. 'We both had a lot of growing up to do,' Jane recalled twenty years later. 'He's been married to four women since, so it wasn't just me.' Her property settlement included oil lands worth half a million dollars, $1,000 monthly in alimony and a $24,000 educational trust fund for the three Moss children.

In October 1955 Jane married for the second time, her

husband being Kenneth Errair, a former member of the Four Freshmen singing group. 'That one was truly meant to be,' said Jane. 'It almost takes one marriage to find out what it's all about.' The family moved back to Hollywood and Jane had two more children, Kenny Jnr and Kendall Jane. Errair was killed in an automobile accident in 1968. Jane's Josephine the Plumber commercials had been undertaken to support his late-blooming ambition to study law. Like all Withers family decisions it was settled at a family council with the children present.

'I told my kids as they were growing up that I had never gone to school with any other kids—Shirley and I each had a private tutor at the studio,' said Jane, 'and that they had to help me along. I was willing to learn but they had to clue me in.' Jane insisted that her daughter wear bobbysox to school, although Wendy claimed no one else did. Jane went to the top of a hill overlooking the school with a pair of binoculars. The next day she said, 'You're right, no more bobbysox, and I'll never doubt you again.'

Wendy, at a certain age, reminded nostalgic filmgoers of Shirley Temple in her heyday, which horrified Jane at first. 'Wendy is going to stay a little girl,' she insisted. 'I was so busy, I missed the wonderful business of growing up. I don't want that for Wendy.' When her elder daughter graduated from high school and still seemed to want to pursue show business, Jane let her audition for the chorus of a dinner theatre show Jane was starring in. Jane coached Wendy through that and a couple of starring parts in stock companies before Wendy decided in favour of marriage herself.

The family council voted unanimously for Jane's full-time comeback in 1974 when she was forty-eight. 'Two years ahead of schedule,' Jane noted at the time. 'I always said I'd come back to it at fifty, after my kids were grown—being a wife and mommy was always number one. But my youngest are seventeen and fourteen now and all five of them knew more at thirteen than I did at twenty-two; they can cope.' She started with guest appearances on Mitzi Gaynor's television special and on *Grammy Salutes Oscar* another special. They had her singing and tap-dancing as she hadn't since she was a teenager. 'I knew all the dances of today, the loose steps, the frug, having chaperoned dances for the kids, but that's all. I hadn't tap-danced for five babies.'

She went to Mitzi's teacher to brush up on singing. 'I've always just sung for pleasure,' Jane said. 'I can't read a note, but I sing in an honest voice. I *care* and I enjoy it. And that's what the teacher thought: "You just keep on doin' what you're doin', you don't need me" he said.' For the Gaynor special, although Jane was singing Peggy Lee's *W-O-M-A-N* among other numbers, the look and style was supposed to be the 1930s. To get the look 'I re-ran my epics, which I hadn't done in a long time—the kids run them all the time, four and five a day. I tell 'em "you don't have to do that, just tell me what you want." '

A perfectionist since childhood, Jane insisted on the same crew each time she did a Josephine commercial—for which she flew to New York four times a year—something that usually just isn't done in the fast world of TV advertising. But when she had made movies at Fox it was 'the Withers Family', the same technical people for each picture, and that's the way it had to be forty years later. Jane also insisted on doing the French-Canadian versions herself, phonetically, rather than having a man's voice over her Josephine image. 'I don't just work to make a buck,' she said. 'I work and work until I get it right.'

All her life, since her mother had taught Sunday School and her father conducted an adult Bible class at the Gordon Street Presbyterian Church back in Atlanta, religion had been the guiding force in Jane's life. A teetotaller and non-smoker she said a silent grace even before business lunches in her regular booth at the Brown Derby outside which she had stood as a six year old. Her strongest expletives were 'Boy howdy' and 'Golly Gussie'. Later she broke from straight Presbyterianism after twenty-six years of perfect church attendance in favour of a more eclectic religious affiliation.

Jane became a trustee of Hollywood's Church of Religious Science. She occasionally attended other churches ranging from Unitarian to Roman Catholic and when in New York she worshipped at the Dutch Reformed Marble Collegiate Church, whose famous pastor Norman Vincent Peale became her close friend. Son Bill, whose wife made Jane a grandmother in September 1974, studied for the ministry in a predominantly Episcopal but multi-denominational seminary in Texas. 'I never had a doubt in my mind that I wouldn't get an answer to my prayers', Jane said, 'and I always ask God's help when there are major decisions to be made. I try to plan my life carefully, but I'm a firm believer that when it's your turn, you'll get it.'

Besides her church work, Jane was an active member of the Hollywood Walk of Fame, which put bronze stars in the sidewalk along Hollywood Boulevard. She was also on the boards of the Cancer Society and the Hollywood Chamber of Commerce, and worked diligently for organisations alleviating cancer, arthritis, tuberculosis, children born without arms and legs, spinal meningitis and withdrawal from narcotics.

'When I was nine years old,' recalled Jane, 'I wanted to be a medical missionary. I didn't think working in movies was involved enough with people. But a very wise man told me, "It's a very important thing to be able to make people laugh at a time when they need it—you can be a missionary of laughter." I've dedicated my life to that.'

For the Hollywood Museum she was spearheading to commemorate the town in which she lived most of that life, Jane bought up 'anything I can get from old movie sets—furniture, china, bric-a-brac'. For years, waiting for the museum to become a reality, at Jane's large house in Hollywood—'built in 1926 just like me'—they had thrones instead of chairs in the living room. In one of them sat, even in 1975, stage mother Lavinia Withers who continued to help answer the telephone and keep track of her daughter's appointments. 'Naturally,' said Jane, 'I'm still her whole life.'

Chapter Four

When she was ten years old Shirley Temple decided to be a Republican, for a 'facetious' reason but one that nonetheless stuck with her throughout her life. On a promotional trip back East she stopped in Boston, where Mayor Curley still held sway. Shirley visited him at City Hall.

'When we came out,' she recalled, 'there were lots of fans around his car and everyone was getting fingerprints on his black limousine, and it made him annoyed. I was leaning out of the car, waving goodbye and Mayor Curley was so upset about all those fans getting fingerprints on his car that when he got in he slammed the door on my four fingers. They're still slightly bent.

'I found out that Mayor Curley was a Democrat and

thought that was a good reason to pick out the other party, so I started early.'

Out in public in the period 1936–1940, Mayor Curley notwithstanding, Shirley was lionised and accorded just about every formal accolade short of an honorary university degree. The week of her eighth birthday in 1936—which the innocent world thought was only her seventh—she became the youngest person ever to appear on the cover of *Time*, and the story inside displayed her forged birth certificate. Also the youngest person ever to be listed in *Who's Who*, Shirley's capsule biography was nineteen lines long, eight longer than Greta Garbo's, the next most prominent from the show business world.

Shirley was also an honorary Kentucky Colonel, a Captain of the Texas Rangers, a member of the staff of the Governor of Idaho, mascot of the Chilean Navy and president of the 400,000-member Chum's Club of Scotland—and of the Kiddies Club of England, whose 165,000 members pledged to imitate her character, conduct and manners. She received 3,500 fan letters a week, 1,100 of them from people over the age of fifty. On New Year's Day 1939, Shirley was Grand Marshall of the Rose Bowl Parade in Pasadena :

'The coldest day of my life,' she recalled, 'we had to get on the floats at four o'clock in the morning.'

The President of the United States, Franklin D. Roosevelt, was 'her willing slave all afternoon' when Shirley visited him in Washington, D.C. in 1937. They talked about, among other things, fishing and the rigours of travel. That same year Mrs Eleanor Roosevelt dropped by the set of *Little Miss Broadway*, intending to stay for about fifteen minutes and watch one of Shirley's dance numbers with George Murphy.

'We immediately fell twenty minutes behind schedule,' Senator Murphy recalled in 1975, 'because as soon as Shirley met somebody she touched them; nobody told her to do it or how to do it, she just did it.'

'Mrs Roosevelt stayed for two hours,' Shirley remembered, 'and then we had lunch together in my bungalow. She invited me to visit her at Hyde Park, New York, where she personally did a barbecue for me. I asked her, "What do you do?" and she told me of her interest in the people of the world and how she was trying to improve the lot of people in my country, and make suggestions to the League of Nations. She made quite an impression on me.'

Apart from the 100,000 feet of film in which she appeared every year, Shirley Temple was the most photographed human being in the world in the mid 1930s, not excluding President Roosevelt or the Duke of Windsor. She was the only American besides Babe Ruth to be universally adored in Japan. And the Greeks had a special word of endearment for her. Since the world's great visited her at the studio Shirley acquired one of the world's great autograph collections.

She seemed to be universally beloved, and an eternally loving personality herself.

At home at playtime Shirley's activities somewhat belied her screen image. For one thing, she was fonder of guns than dolls. 'I had a Roy Rogers flare gun, cap pistols, everything,' she said. She told a visitor who turned out to be the president of a gun factory of her interest, and he sent her an air rifle— 'But I only got a glimpse of it. I was a tomboy back in Santa Monica. We had four acres of wild forest around us. I had a horse and a neighbourhood gang, mostly boys. I was a blue-jeans and T-shirt kind of little girl. I climbed trees, took archery and swam a lot.'

In keeping with those interests, one of her favourite movies was the 1937 *Wee Willie Winkie*, based loosely on the Rudyard Kipling story, directed by John Ford and of course originally conceived for a boy. 'In it I was a real bossy girl,' she said. 'I marched, drilled, did the manual of arms. I had a wooden gun. It was wonderful. I wanted to join the FBI and be the first woman G-man; in fact, J. Edgar Hoover made me one.' She in turn organised the Shirley Temple Police Force and inducted Hoover, Mrs Roosevelt and all cast and crew members on all her pictures. There were fines for not wearing the badges and not keeping them brightly shined, the dues from which later built boys' and girls' clubs in Santa Monica.

Shirley also went through a period, when she was seven, of wanting to be a pie-seller. 'My parents were building a new house,' she said, 'and I would take pie tins and fill them with cement to sell to the tourists who would come by the house. Of course they wanted a pie that had been made by Shirley Temple, but I thought they really wanted them. I believed in what I was selling. There was no false advertising at all, no handprint in them or anything. They were just plain old cement pies. That job lasted a couple of days until my mother got wind of it. I made five cents a pie.'

The Shirley Temple pictures of the 1936-40 period continued to set box-office records. And while all were star vehicles specifically invented or adapted for her, *Captain January*, her first release in 1936—and the first since the reorganisation of the $54 million Twentieth Century-Fox of which she was the single most valuable asset—turned out to be one of the best movies she ever made. Based on the 1890 Laura E. Richards story *The Lighthouse at Cape Tempest*, *Captain January* was the story of a poor foundling named Star (Shirley) who was washed up on the New England seashore and taken in by a kindly lighthouse keeper (Guy Kibbee), but pursued by a truant officer. 'Cap! Cap! I don't want to go!' Shirley-Star shouted, as she did in variations on that phrase in most of her films.

Her songs in *Captain January* included *Early Bird* with which she awoke in the morning, and *The Right Somebody to Love*. A dance with Buddy Ebsen, *At the Codfish Ball*, is among the best numbers she did in film. A camera tracked along a wooden street following the pair as they danced over stacks of boxes and barrels and up and down wooden stairs. During the filming of this sequence, Shirley had to climb a forty-five foot stairway while a camera crane moved up beside her, catching her lines each time she turned on the stairs, timing the line exactly to the turn. Shirley never missed the synchronisation once. With Kibbee and Slim Summerville, Shirley did a three-part version of the sextet from *Lucia*—the star's mother had, in fact, been an opera singer.

Ebsen, as TV's *Barnaby Jones* in 1975, remembered himself as 'the new boy in town and Shirley the established star' in *Captain January* and recalled learning film technique from her. She was still telling corny jokes—'There are three holes in the ground ... well, well, well!'—but she was supremely aware of her position on the Fox lot. Some journalists were interviewing Gertrude Temple, Mrs Withers and other movie mothers and guardians one day when Shirley sauntered over to say : 'Why don't you talk to me? I'm the star.'

She was vain enough about her prestige that when a child bit player in *Captain January*, Jerry Tucker, was getting applause on the set for a good job of acting in a schoolroom scene, Shirley sat on a small chair out of camera range, her eyes flashing with jealousy. Her scene following his was a full page of dialogue. As with all long speeches David Butler, the director, had planned to break the scene between a medium shot and a close-up. But when Shirley began her speech Butler let the camera run through the entire long monologue, which Shirley, to regain her position, was delivering without a mis-

53

take. In fact, Shirley's only problem in *Captain January* was that her baby teeth kept falling out and she had to wear temporary false caps on camera.

On the release of *Captain January* in early 1936 critics divided as they always did on Shirley Temple movies. 'Neither epic, romance, nor extravaganza,' *Time* wrote, 'it is designed solely as its star's vehicle. As an item of entertainment *Captain January* depends entirely upon the fact that Shirley Temple appears in almost every sequence, grinning, sobbing, dancing, singing, wriggling, pattering downstairs or spitting on her pinafore as the scenario requires. That this is entirely as it should be, in the opinion of U.S. cinema addicts was proved by the reception of the picture. *Captain January* smashed box-office records in Milwaukee, Portland, Me., Dayton, Richmond, Cincinatti, Boston and Baltimore.'

Frank Nugent of *The New York Times*, however, denounced the movie's 'moss-covered script'. He didn't like Shirley's June 1936 release, *Poor Little Rich Girl*, any better, and he lamented unnecessarily on behalf of co-stars Jack Haley and Alice Faye : 'Short of becoming a defeated candidate for vice president, we can think of no better method of guaranteeing one's anonymity than appearing in the moppet's films.' And, in October, Nugent denounced *Dimples* even more vehemently. 'The Shirley Temple for President Club reconvened yesterday and displayed flattering attention to their candidate's latest assault upon the nation's maternal instinct,' Nugent wrote in his *Times* review, '*Dimples* is its apt title, apt because it is just another word for Little Miss Precocity and does not pretend to describe the story material it employs. Why they bother with titles or with plots either, is beyond us.'

Actually, *Poor Little Rich Girl*, which had a lot less plot than Pickford's 1916 version, had some good songs Shirley's *When I'm With You* and *Oh My Goodness* and Alice's *But Definitely* and, in the making, came the first indication that

Shirley was less than a perfect performer. *I Love A Military Man*, an obviously tacked-on tap number, was a little fast and intricate even for Shirley and Jack Haley remembered that 'they dubbed in Shirley's taps but didn't tell Mrs Temple. They shot it with her, then told Alice and me to come back later and do it again. At the preview Mrs Temple was boasting, "Did you hear those taps? Could they have been any clearer? And you said Shirley couldn't do it." '

In *Dimples*, which was set in New York City in 1850 and which tried for a Dickensian flavour in the original Nunnally Johnson screenplay, Shirley was upstaged for the first time in one of her starring pictures. Frank Morgan, later the Wizard of Oz, played her Micawberesque grandfather with such energy and fun as to render Shirley, as the street urchin who becomes a Broadway star, faltering and hollow. The unabated box-office success of *Dimples*, however, caused Zanuck and the rest of Fox to worry less about the money crisis occasioned by Will Rogers' death in a plane crash.

The Stowaway, her last film in 1936, had Shirley an orphan again, the daughter of missionaries in China who were killed by bandits. For the picture she learned and spoke Mandarin Chinese. Her co-stars were Robert Young and Alice Faye, who had two of the film's excellent songs: *Goodnight My Love* and *One Never Knows, Does One?* Shirley promoted the on-screen romance between Young and Faye, and did imitations of Eddie Cantor, Ginger Rogers (with a male doll in black tie attached to her toes) and Al Jolson. The picture cleaned up.

In 1937, although she only made two films, *Wee Willie Winkie* and *Heidi* she was number one at the box office for the third year in a row. 'What's to become of Shirley Temple is one of the burning issues of the movie industry,' the one-year-old *Life* magazine worried that year. 'She has lost some of her early prettiness and all of her babyish cuteness, but has gained enough acting tricks to leave her with a full quota of charm.' But Shirley was now nearly four feet tall—against three feet-two inches in 1934—and her hair was soon to be parted into two pony tails, another sign of advancing age.

Zanuck conceived the notion of pairing her with John Ford in the Kipling story. Her three strong male co-stars were Victor McLaglen, Cesar Romero and C. Aubrey Smith. Her favourites remained, however, her first : James Dunn, Bill Robinson, and Gary Cooper, who called her 'Wigglebritches'— 'He was so tall I barely ever talked to him unless he was sitting down, he was so kind and bashful.' Shirley not only liked the picture for its military flavour, she liked Ford. 'Outwardly he is a rugged person,' she said, 'but inside he's kindly and even sentimental.'

Ford, who after working with her gave her the sobriquet 'One-Take Temple' recalled how Zanuck had begun to tamper with the formula for Shirley's movies : 'One day Darryl said, "I'm going to give you something to scream about. I'm going to put you together with Shirley Temple." He thought that combination would make me and everybody howl. I said, "Great," and we just went out and made the picture. It made a lot of money.' Ford and Temple stayed friends until his death and he became Susan's godfather.

Zanuck, for his part, while believing in general that pictures were more important than stars, thought, 'Shirley Temple is endless. There's no one in the world to compare with that child. I've made eight pictures with her, and each time I'm knocked dead. It's just beyond the case of being a freak. This child has rhythm. I always thought when we dropped the curls—this is the end. This mint, this gold mine has gone dry. But now she's good for years.' His optimism aside, Zanuck increased the budgets on her films and gave her stronger supporting casts.

Heidi, with Allan Dwan directing and the gifted Jean

Hersholt playing her grandfather, could have been written for Shirley Temple, although Dwan jazzed up and desentimentalised the Johanna Spyri Swiss classic with low comedy tricks and a high costume dream sequence. *Rebecca of Sunnybrook Farm*, another Mary Pickford remake which was directed by Dwan, who had also directed Pickford in the 1915 *A Girl of Yesterday*, found the original story in a shambles but Shirley at the top of her form. 'Any actress who can dominate a Zanuck musical with Jack Haley, Gloria Stuart, Phyllis Brooks, Helen Westley, Slim Summerville, Bill Robinson, Randolph Scott, Franklin Pangborn, etc. can dominate the world,' *Variety* wrote.

Rebecca left no stone unturned when it came to milking the old Shirley Temple formula. Her new songs included *Come and Get Your Happiness* and the film's finale was a tap dance with Bill Robinson done to *The Parade of the Wooden Soldiers*, and both veterans were in snappy form. She sang, in the guise of Rebecca making her radio debut, a medley of her earlier hits, including *On the Good Ship Lollipop* and *When I'm With You!*

Little Miss Broadway was written just for Shirley, even to the point of explaining her new hair-do : 'I used to have curls all over my head but they were a lot of trouble,' read a line of her dialogue. There was no explaining her new seventy-one-pound plumpness, and four-foot-three-inch height, but fortunately the movie also had George Murphy dancing a beautiful duet with her to *We Should Be Together*, and Edna May Oliver, Jimmy Durante and *Swing Me An Old-Fashioned Song* to enliven it. Murphy recalled in 1975 that during filming Shirley 'would pop out of the damndest places to see if you had your police badge on and raised between $2000-3,000 from 25-cent fines.' He also remembered 'giving her' their scenes together. 'Some of the critics mentioned this, but I never tried to compete; I always deferred to her.'

While she was still child enough to be excited because there was a flood at Fox during filming 'and nobody was gonna be allowed to leave the studio', Shirley, in Murphy's memory, was 'nearly adult and perfectly natural in her reactions; her emotions were real and the director never seemed to have problems with her.' When she was deciding whether or not to run for Congress in 1967, she visited Murphy in Los Angeles to ask his advice. 'Her potential campaign was just as well-organised as she had been in pictures, and I told her her good common sense would be an asset in Congress.'

Dwan recalled in 1974 at the age of eighty-nine that when he first met Shirley 'she was waning. She'd had her peak and was sliding fast. Zanuck would like to have made a trade but nobody was interested, and I liked to avoid children especially those who were over. In a kind of left-handed way he gave me *Heidi* and said, 'See what you can do with it.' *Heidi's* a very down story, stiff and heavy, but Zanuck loosened the purse strings a little. We got to use Lake Arrowhead locations for the Alps—and a lot of tricks. She helped invent the dream sequence where she's in Holland because she thought that way—she knew it was a good spot for a musical number.'

Gertrude Temple, however, in Dwan's view, was the real creative genius. 'Shirley was the product of her mother,' he said. 'Shirley was the instrument on which her mother played. I don't know why the mother was like that—but I'd seen it before with Mary Pickford and her domineering mother. As a director, whenever I wanted anything from Shirley I looked at the mother.'

Dwan served for his three pictures with Shirley—including the 1940 *Young People*—as Captain of the Shirley Temple Police Force; Shirley, of course, was Chief. For years he kept a supply of badges and whenever he was stopped for speeding he would whip one out. Though it was a fake and she was passé, the gift of one to a policeman usually prevented a ticket.

During *Rebecca* he made the mistake of getting Gene Krupa to supply her with a 'perfect set of drums. Her rhythm was good on those, too, but for several days we didn't get any work done.'

Shirley was such a perfect mimic that she could unconsciously pick up an accent like Bill Robinson's as easily as she did his dance steps. 'I'd have to tell Mrs Temple to stop it—we were in talking pictures. But it was such a pleasure working with her—I never saw her anger or annoy anyone— that it was a shame to take the money. It was sad that the spark lasted only to a certain age. But if Shirley Temple was only a moment in movie history, it was a great moment.'

Shirley's (or Mrs Temple's) instrument—unlike a Stradivarius —was clearly not improving with age. *Just Around the Corner*, her last film of 1938, foundered at the box office despite help from Bert Lahr, Joan Davis, Charles Farrell, Franklin Panghorn and a final Temple-Robinson dance duet, *I Love to Walk in the Rain*. Shirley even tried a Jane Withers ploy and acted out one of her fantasies by pummelling her picture playmates with a toy machine gun as she said, 'I guess that'll teach you a lesson; you can't fool a G-woman.'

She still ended up box-office champ in 1938, but at the start of the next year the studio turned to Technicolor and a big budget ($1.5 million) to shore up their falling star. *The Little Princess*, yet another Pickford silent triumph, and based on the novel by Frances Hodgson Burnett, was set in England in 1899.

Arthur Treacher, a frequent co-star and the proto-typical butler, sang and danced with Shirley; Anita Louise and Richard Greene were on hand for romantic interest; and even Queen Victoria was dragged into the proceedings. Its beautiful photography and quality production values got *The Little Princess* critical attention, but the box-office success in the children's fantasy department in 1939 was *The Wizard of Oz* and Judy Garland was the future as Shirley Temple was the past. Ironically, Shirley had been considered for the *Wizard* two years before.

Susannah of the Mounties, Shirley's second film of 1939, was a romantic melodrama also starring Randolph Scott, Margaret Lockwood, J. Farrell MacDonald and Victor Jory. It was the last film to make money in her seven-year association with Twentieth Century-Fox and it took in enough— along with *The Little Princess* and hold-over revenues from 1938—to keep Shirley from sinking no further than fifth place in the box-office standing. At the age of eleven, she was given a pre-adolescent, semi-romantic interest in Martin Good Rider, a pure-blooded Blackfoot Indian boy. Her mini-squaw character in this banal tale of the North-West was unsympathetic and she was limited to one pathetic song and dance : *I'll Teach You A Waltz.*

In 1940 *The Blue Bird*, based on Maurice Maeterlinck's 1905 play was a Technicolor fantasy that some saw as Fox's answer to *The Wizard of Oz*, but it was deadly—in two senses of the word—and dated. Temple herself thought it was ahead of its time, and others thought so as well; in 1975 it was remade with Elizabeth Taylor, Jane Fonda, Cicely Tyson and others in a U.S.-U.S.S.R. co-production in Leningrad directed by George Cukor. The Temple version, however, lost money— her first film to do so.

Young People not only took her back to the familiar orphan and the vaudeville couple format, but under Dwan's direction it shamelessly used clips of musical numbers from Shirley's previous films. Jack Oakie, Charlotte Greenwood and the songs *Strolling on the Avenue* and *I Wouldn't Take A Million* gave *Young People* some vitality, but Shirley was simply too old at twelve to be a cute child and too young to be an interesting young woman.

Fittingly, *Young People* was about a little girl who grows up and tries to become just like other girls. George and Gertrude Temple bought up the remainder of Shirley's contract from Fox and sent her off to a real school. Shirley had stopped believing in Santa Claus when one in a department store asked for her autograph, and had worn her first long dress at her eleventh birthday party. She took the decision stoically.

Chapter Five

Westlake School for Girls in Los Angeles was an exclusive, expensive country day school and as close to an Eastern 'prep' school as anything in California when Shirley enrolled there in 1940, aged twelve. Her parents put her there, she said thirty-five years later, 'so that I would know what competition was. I spent the first year in that school looking at all the other girls' hairstyles, and they told me all the latest jokes. I grew up rapidly once I got into that school. At the studio I hadn't had much to do with the other children because we were working and they were with their tutors also.'

Shirley was not retiring from movies, Gertrude carefully explained, but until she was through with school her time at work would be limited and the properties carefully chosen. No new contracts were signed but rumours were plentiful. MGM and Hal Roach were said to want her for term contracts and Universal, Columbia and independent producer Lester Cowan were offering single pictures—Cowan's supposedly was *Cosmopolitan*, an F. Scott Fitzgerald story. Mrs Temple turned down three Broadway musicals, including an *Uncle Tom's Cabin* in swingtime and Cole Porter's *Dubarry*

Was A Lady staring Ethel Merman, but was open to a radio deal.

Along with other girls at school, Shirley listened to President Roosevelt's defence message in the spring of 1940, made notes and talked about it with her family when she got home. But war talk in general upset her since brothers Jack, aged twenty-five, a graduate student at Stanford, and George, twenty-one, at home in Brentwood, were very vulnerable to the draft. Her preferred radio fare consisted of serials like *Orphan Annie* and *Superman* from 5.30–6.30 pm when the four Temples sat down to dinner. And even on the road, all activity ceased when *The Lone Ranger* hit the airwaves.

Shirley spent her summer vacation between seventh and eighth grades at Westlake taking swimming lessons, pecking away at a typewriter with no special writing to do, and playing with her girlfriends Mary Lou Islieb and Harold Lloyd's daughters Peggy and Gloria. Sometimes she made as many as three daily trips to the main gate in front of the Temple compound to give out autographs and wave to the tour buses. She superintended the building of her elaborate playhouse, whose architecture was English lodge house. Its main feature was a small theatre with a proscenium stage and velvet curtains at one end, and seats for eighty-five people. The auditorium could be converted for dancing. There were also special rooms for her doll collection, unanswered fan mail, and games. A regulation duck-pin bowling alley was in the basement. On her three trips to Honolulu, Shirley had delightedly discovered slot machines, and one was included there too.

She had given up riding six months before when two girlfriends were killed in accidents with horses, and the Temples sold her two ponies and her horse, which had been stabled in the backyard. Fox's chairman Nicholas Schenk had imported a Shetland pony from the Shetland Islands as a present for her—needless to say, before the acrimony between Fox and the Temples over the end of Shirley's contract—and it remained as an unridden pet, along with three small dogs. The Temples kept a cook and maid, and a chauffeur to drive Shirley to work or school in a Pontiac station wagon. Her only professional appearance in several months was on a Red Cross coast-to-coast radio broadcast in which Shirley did a melodramatic skit with Paul Muni.

However, old habits die hard, and by late 1941, Shirley Temple was back at work. She did four shows for Lux soap at $5,000 per show and a four-part *Shirley Temple Time for Elgin* at the same salary. On the first of the Elgin shows the announcer introduced Shirley as "America's Little Sweetheart', and it seemed for a while that the build-up was on to place her on Mary Pickford's long unoccupied throne. (Pickford and Temple had been photographed together the year before as a couple of 'has-beens'.) During the dress rehearsal Shirley had induced a few sentimental tears from the audience, but dressed in blue velveteen, squinching her nose, smiling sweetly and throwing off virginal vibrations as a five-foot, one hundred-pound thirteen years old, her actual on-the-air reading of lines left the audience dry-eyed.

Mama Temple, as before, was in back-up attendance at the broadcast and George Snr. announced that there were 'half a dozen more good offers'. Shirley herself said about radio : 'It's adorable. I get a big thrill out of it and I want to do as much radio work as I can. I like it because you have to do it right the first time. In pictures if it's wrong you can do it over.'

More rumours of movie work for Shirley circulated, most prominently that she would sing with fellow teens Deanna Durbin and Gloria Jean at Universal for producer Joseph Pasternak. Louis B. Mayer at MGM signed her for her comeback at a salary of $50,000 per picture or $2,500 a week, humiliating when stacked against her last salary for Fox,

*Shirley's Christmases were always shared
with her adoring public, who were given
a detailed listing of her presents; this is a
1938 studio publicity shot.*

(Above)
In 1939's **The Little Princess**
Shirley's co-stars were Anita
Louise (behind her, to the left)
and Arthur Treacher.

(Below)
In the original movie made of
Maeterlinck's **The Blue Bird**
in 1939-40, Shirley played Mytel.
It was Twentieth Century Fox's
answer to Judy Garland in
The Wizard of Oz.

*A junior shutterbug on the set of **Young People** in 1940, Shirley was already at the awkward looking, twelve-year-old stage and past her box-office prime.*

(Above)
In 1943, when she was fifteen and
Mary Pickford was fifty, **Life**
Magazine called them 'has-beens'.
(Credit: Fred Parrish for Life.)

(Below right)
At sixteen Shirley became an
ingenue for David O. Selznick
in **Since You Went Away**.

Graduation from Westlake in 1945.

John Agar was Shirley's favourite
serviceman . . . and first husband,
1945.

*Shirley and John Agar's reception was
in the Temple backyard, 1947.*

(Above)
André De Dienes, the
photographer who discovered
Marilyn Monroe, tried to make
Shirley sexy but the public
wouldn't have it. (Credit:
André De Dienes)

(Below right)
Shirley did her bit to boost morale
during World War II at the famous
Hollywood Canteen.

$300,000 for the film or $9,000 a week. No longer blonde or chubby, Shirley posed for publicity stills with MGM's top stars Mickey Rooney and Judy Garland with an announcement that the three juveniles would appear together in *Babes In Arms*, and in the Andy Hardy series.

But her actual come-back movie was *Kathleen*, the making of which in the summer and autumn of 1941, Shirley described as being 'like a wonderful vacation—no school or anything, just fun, like it used to be'. On release, Shirley's work in *Kathleen* was praised ('An appealing young lady of quiet charm and impressive assurance,' wrote a national reviewer) but the modest picture came off as just another remake of *Poor Little Rich Girl*. Shirley played the miserable daughter of a widower (Herbert Marshall) who neglects her. She gets rid of her rotten governess and her father's featherbrained fiancée (Gail Patrick) and marries Daddy off to the new nice governess (Laraine Day). Shirley wasn't an awkward thirteen, but a self-assured actress who seemed to be embarrassed by the banal script. The MGM contract was cancelled by mutual consent.

Her second come-back film was no better. *Miss Annie Rooney*, a low-budget rehash released through United Artists, was notable only in that it contained her first screen kiss from a contemporary, a chaste peck on the cheek—'It felt like a butterfly; it tickled,' she said—from Dickie Moore that was widely ballyhooed. Shirley was given a lot of 1942 jive talk to say ('how divinely snaky') and pleated jumpers and saddle-shoes to wear. But everything else about the picture was sadly out of date, and so wrong for Shirley that she retired again for almost two years.

Shirley was at Westlake enough of the time to sustain a B-average, and there she threw herself into the role of a snappy wartime teenager of her day. She participated in freshman hazing, wearing a sunbonnet and shining seniors'

shoes with a toothbrush for a week, and went to dances in long
dresses with military academy boys. She wore an ankle
bracelet, and too much lipstick—except when her mother lay
'in wait for me, brandishing a Kleenex', which was most of
the time. She also wore a standard navy blue Westlake
uniform except that she had wide Adrian-style shoulders
added. 'Got to have some glamour,' she explained.

Still, the Temples and Shirley were serious about a come-
back and she took voice lessons and studied with drama
coach Robert Graham Paris. Paris escorted her one night in
1943 to the Hollywood Canteen, the U.S.O.'s star-studded
haven for servicemen on leave in the Los Angeles area. Mrs
John Ford was in charge and Bette Davis had suggested
Shirley to sell kisses. Shirley, in spite of all the concern for her
safety, which included being ushered in through the kitchen,
stayed to jitterbug the night away with nary an assault on her
fifteen-year-old person.

'Shirley was never allowed to know that she was anything
special,' Paris recalled just before his death in 1974, 'even in
her "adult" movie years. She was still asked to do chores like
making beds and not to behave like a star—Jane Withers, on
the other hand, was encouraged to run around with a
Hollywood crowd. The Temples were the most normal of
families in a town full of abnormal families. Shirley didn't
really become a woman during those years. She didn't become
a woman until she became a politician.'

David O. Selznick, who already had Ingrid Bergman, Joan
Fontaine, Jennifer Jones and Joseph Cotten under contract,
signed Shirley Temple to a seven-year personal contract in
1944 and announced as her first vehicle *Since You Went
Away*, his self-written tribute to the American Family in
wartime. Selznick billed Shirley only fourth—after Claudette
Colbert, Jones and Cotten—and was anxious to have the film

regarded as another major star-studded Selznick epic, his first since *Gone With the Wind*, and not as a vehicle for Temple's comeback. But, in spite of his best efforts to the contrary, *Since You Went Away* was, in large part at least, just that.

Shirley wore high heels and breezed through the part of the midteen 'Brig', Claudette's daughter and Jennifer's kid sister. 'I knew all about her right from the beginning,' said Shirley, 'because she was practically me.' She worked well with Monty Woolley, the household's crusty lodger, and with Cotten and Robert Walker as young servicemen. Even Lionel Barrymore, a co-star of her youth, was on hand for a cameo role as a fire-and-brimstone minister. The picture was instantly popular and remained an outstanding glimpse of the American homefront in World War II.

Quickly, Selznick cast Shirley in a lower budget but still stylish companion piece to *Since You Went Away*. Again the setting was wartime and Cotten played the romantic male lead. Ginger Rogers was his romantic interest and Shirley played her little sister—and third lead, this time. 'I had a tremendous crush on Joseph Cotten,' she recalled. 'I thought he was just perfect. He had a charming manner and treated me as a sixteen-year-old should be treated : as an equal. I would be a little shy when I wasn't supposed to be. When they said they were going to get married or whatever I had to throw my arms around his neck. I remember it was very exciting at the time.'

Selznick gave Shirley a Sweet Sixteen birthday party on the set of *Since You Went Away*—but during filming of *Double Furlough*—thus continuing the tradition that began when she was five but which hadn't been observed for three years. Because of the war the party was kept deliberately simple, and lasted exactly one hour. Its total cost was $46.11 : cake, $24, five gallons of vanilla ice cream, $17.50 and three boxes of candy, $4.61. Members of the cast and crew gave Shirley roses and Selznick gave her a silver bracelet with a heart attached.

All other gifts were gags. Ginger Rogers gave Shirley a John Fredericks hat made of chicken feathers, while Cotten presented her with a box of paper balls that exploded and jumped when the lid opened. Monty Woolley's gift was a copy of *Life Begins at Forty*. Mary Lou Islieb, who was still Shirley's stand-in, gave her a dribbling water glass, Jennifer Jones a make-up book and Tom Tully a rubber hot dog—the real kind being Shirley's favourite food. Dare Harris, who was seventeen and one of Shirley's dates, gave her a fake newspaper front page with the headline: 'SHIRLEY TEMPLE WILL BE 65 IN 1993.'

Mrs Temple gave her daughter just what she needed, another doll (an antique French one) and 'Joy' perfume, Shirley's favourite. Mr Temple came up with more 'Joy', a gold pin and an Eversharp fountain pen. Brother Jack sent flowers and classical record albums. Shirley's dress for the occasion was a grey chiffon over pink with a bodice of cut embroidery and came from the wardrobe of a new film in the making—which was also called *With All My Heart* until Selznick acquired the rights to the popular song *I'll Be Seeing You* to use in the movie.

Despite her advanced years, and having achieved her full adult height of five-foot-two, Shirley was still required to have three hours of school on the set and one hour of recreation—walking, reading, talking with friends—before 4 pm. Lunch had to be at 12.30 and she had to be off the set by 6 pm. Shirley had a much freer choice in her clothing and social life. She sometimes went on dates without chaperons and was allowed to use the Temple car and chauffeur. Dare Harris, who was in the movie (having been discovered by a Selznick talent scout in a bowling alley) was not Shirley's favourite date—he wasn't in uniform, after all. But he was ardent in his pursuit, once following the Temples to Palm Springs and camping out in the desert because there were no available hotel rooms.

The two wartime Temple-Selznick films were released in rapid succession and Selznick was excited by the reaction to Shirley Temple. In one of the producer's famous memos, he wrote at the end of 1944: 'Shirley is exceedingly hot at the moment. We can't commence to fill demands for interviews and other press material on her from newspapers and magazines; and this is, of course, an indication of the interest of the public. At the preview of *I'll Be Seeing You* ... Shirley's name was received with the biggest applause of all three (stars) despite the fact that the Gallup poll shows that Cotten is the great new romantic rage, and that Ginger is one of the top stars of the business.

'Shirley's publicity in the New York press, both in connection with this appearance and in connection with her prior trip East to sell bonds, received more publicity—including, astonishingly, big front-page breaks in the middle of a war—than I think has been accorded the visit of any motion-picture star to New York in many, many years ... Her fan mail is greater than that of any other star on our list—actually exceeding by a wide margin that of Ingrid Bergman, Jennifer Jones and Joan Fontaine, who are the next three in that order ..."

For all that, the producer soon became preoccupied with Jennifer Jones, who, divorcing Robert Walker, would later marry Selznick, and he lost interest in developing the career of a second ingenue. While he kept Shirley under contract the rest of her films would be with her on loan to other studios, and the sequence began with the screen version of the Broadway success *Kiss And Tell*.

In the movie script, Shirley as Corliss Archer runs a U.S.O. charity bazaar stocked with hand-embroidered guest towels.

Business is non-existent until she persuades her boyfriend to buy five towels for five dollars. In gratitude she kisses him and several servicemen standing by assume she is selling kisses and form a line. The scene required 150 atmosphere players including 22 kissers who had their day pay rates adjusted upward for the 'business' they were doing. The kissers were specially selected clean-cut young men, certified for their roles by a male nurse who took temperatures and sprayed their throats (one boy was rejected for garlic on the breath). Mrs Temple naturally reserved the right of veto of any candidate, but didn't exercise it.

Shirley, who admitted only to kissing on celebrations like New Year's Eve, threw herself into the bussings, retake after retake. 'Of course I'll kiss them on the mouth,' she said. 'That's the only kind of kisses worth paying for—kisses on the cheek are just gratuities.' Her private philosophy, she allowed, was that 'a girl shouldn't kiss a boy the first time they're out together—despite the current speed-up.' Gertrude Temple, standing by as always, made her own observation: 'I don't ordinarily get to see Shirley kissing. It is very interesting.'

Chapter Six

When she turned seventeen, in 1945, Shirley had been a film
star for eleven years; her every move had been chronicled
for millions of adoring fans, even during the Westlake School
years and her recent return to films in supporting roles. Still,
she yearned for a more normal American lifestyle, and she
tried very hard to attain it. Much too hard, it turned out. 'I
made a lot of decisions when I was seventeen,' she recalled in
her forties. 'One of them was to get married, and I did. I
wanted marriage more than a career, because you can get
awfully lonely with your scrapbooks when you find yourself
at the end of your career. What it's really all about is marriage and family as far as I'm concerned.'

Graduation from Westlake School for Girls came first,
three months before her wedding in September. 'It was a
beautiful June morning,' she remembered, 'and we all wore
long white dresses down to the ground and carried bouquets
of red roses, all identical. The dresses were alike so no one
would look different from anyone else; we all bought them at
the same place. V-J day was in August of 1945, so the war
was almost at an end, and we were looking forward to all of

our friends—sometimes very close friends—coming back from military service.

'And we were looking forward to the end of petrol rationing and butter rationing and meatless Tuesdays and all the things that were part of the war years. Petrol rationing was the hardest part for us teenagers. We liked to go around in cars, and we'd have to plan very carefully how far we could go an half a tank of petrol, or a quarter of a tank. Very often we'd have to turn off the motor and coast down hills and carefully start again at the bottom. That was the biggest hazard in dating, besides getting home on time,' she said.

One of the most normal things about Shirley in her teens during World War II was that she was boy-crazy. Ever since her first little-girl crushes on her male co-stars, Shirley had reserved her most special affection for the men in her life, something that would later stand her in exceptionally good stead in the mostly-male world of international diplomacy. She dated frequently—co-star Guy Madison and songwriter Nacio Herb Brown, among others—and retained her greatest fondness for men in uniform. And the one returning service-man most likely to keep her out late was John Agar.

Agar, one of the heirs to a Chicago meat-packing family, was a sergeant in the Army Air Force and a physical training instructor at California's March Field. He was handsome, blond, six feet two, and had first met Shirley in 1943 at a tea given by Zasu Pitts, the Temples' next-door neighbour in Brentwood. In the early spring of 1945, even before Shirley's seventeenth birthday, 'Jack' Agar and Shirley Temple decided to get married. He presented her with a dazzling two-and-a-half carat square-cut diamond, which she wore under a glove on her left hand at an April Sunday luncheon in a Beverly Hills restaurant for the forty-three members of the senior class at Westlake.

She thoughtlessly took off the glove and when her schoolmates questioned her about the diamond, Shirley fled, flustered, to the ladies' room. All forty-two girls followed her, giggling, and soon the whole restaurant knew what was going on. Later that afternoon at her parents' home Shirley dimpled a lot, and told the hastily summoned reporters that what she liked most about Jack was his 'sincerity'. The senior Temples, who had not wanted even to announce the engagement at least until Shirley had graduated from high school, nervously added : 'Shirley and John have promised not to get married for two years, possibly three.'

Shirley's birthday was two weeks after the engagement announcement. She spent a quiet day with John and a quiet evening with him and some friends who shared her cake. The next afternoon, however, was turned over to a promotional birthday party fostered by the United National Clothing Collection. On the purported grounds that Shirley was a big girl now and interested in international problems, the organisation talked Mrs Temple into parting with many of Shirley's little-girl dresses, including a few from the films, and most with her name tags still in them. Some of the dresses Gertrude 'just couldn't bear to part with. After all,' she explained, 'there might be a little girl in the family sometime and wouldn't she like to wear some of the things that her mother once wore in pictures?'

Still, some seventy-five garments were piled on a big chair in the Brentwood library and the press was invited in. The press release for the event said that Shirley had decided her first 'adult' good deed would be to help the thirty million children in war-devastated countries. 'It makes me happy to have a part in rebuilding the lives of girls my age or younger,' she said. The hand-out stated: 'Shirley Temple is vitally interested in the future peace of the world and believes that through the United National Clothing Collection every American has the privilege of helping to fashion this peace.'

73

There was another seventeen-candle cake, and almost an hour of posing with clothing drive posters, her dimples and diamond flashing, before John—as previously scheduled—called her on the telephone.

The promises to her parents notwithstanding, Shirley Jane Temple became Mrs John G. Agar at 8.59 pm on the evening of 19 September 1945. Six hundred guests, including California's Governor Earl Warren (whose arrival delayed the 8.30 starting time) and David O. Selznick, witnessed the twelve-minute, double-ring Episcopal ceremony at the Wilshire Methodist Church. Except for Miss Pitts, who came solely in her capacity as next-door neighbour and friend, there were no film stars in attendance, and George and Gertrude tried to keep the proceedings—within limits—dignified. Family and school friends, important members of the press and cameramen and crew from Shirley's early pictures, in evening clothes and furs, predominated.

They arched on tiptoe and craned their necks to see little Shirley, dressed in white satin and preceded by sixteen attendants, march down the aisle on George Snr's arm, playing this latest role with her usual poise, grace and dignity. Her dress had a fitted bodice, short sleeves and a 'Little Infanta' skirt; the low round neck was edged by a looped cord of satin closely studded with seed pearls, with seed pearls also spattered over the bodice. The head-dress holding her veils was a crown of corded satin wired in small loops. Her train was full and long, and the wrist-length satin gloves were scalloped and embroidered with seed pearls. She carried a bouquet of bovardia and white orchids; and a lace handkerchief for something borrowed, a small garter for something blue, a small cross worn inside her dress for something old, and Jack's wedding ring for something new. For good luck she put a penny in her shoe.

Jack Temple's wife was matron of honour and she and

the seven bridesmaids (who included Phoebe Hearst and Mary Lou Isleib, Shirley's stand-in and best friend) wore dresses and cartwheel hats of 'Temple Blue', a new colour named by designer Louella Brantingham. The altar of the church was banked with pink and red roses and several tall candelabra. The centre aisle was ribboned off in blue and groupings of green ferns were sporadically placed around the church. During the actual wedding vows, Shirley kept looking up at John, but displayed no other emotion. Both bride and groom stayed calm.

Several thousand fans who had begun gathering at noon, crammed outside the church, pushed against the ring of military and local police who were trying to keep them roped off, and turned the relatively quiet affair into a Hollywood wedding, reminiscent of the Vilma Banky–Rod LaRoque nuptials in 1927. Little boys trying to achieve a vantage point shinned up every lamp post they could find. For blocks in all directions cars were parked bumper to bumper. When Shirley and John tried to leave the church and pose on the steps for photographers, the crowd surged forth in tidal-wave fashion forcing the couple to retreat into the church for fifteen minutes until the police could again rope off the hordes. In the meantime Shirley refused one woman an autograph, saying she couldn't write with her gloves on.

In front of the Temple home in Brentwood, flagstone flooring was especially laid for the reception. A white three-tiered cake was on display, roped off under a canopy. Under a larger canopy in the centre of the lawn small tables were grouped for eating and drinking, and the wedding party greeted well-wishers under still a third tent on the sidelines. A gypsy orchestra wandered through the 600-strong crowd. David Selznick was very visible, usually among the nubile bridesmaids. Once the actual ceremony was over, the wedding became a David O. Selznick production in the grand manner.

75

Photographers were issued passes (one to a magazine or agency) by his publicity office to get past police lines and were promised, and had delivered to them, the bridal party for fifteen minutes at the church and thirty minutes at home before the reception, for pictures.

While John and Shirley received, their guests consumed twenty cases of Cresta Blanca champagne and countless platters of hors d'oeuvres. They visited Shirley's palatial former playhouse on the property, now containing nine long banquet tables full of wedding presents. The presents ranged from a Capeheart radio console from Selznick and sheer table linen from the Darryl Zanucks to can openers, a frying pan, three cookbooks, and two dozen roses from the San José Fire Department. Mrs Agar gave the newlyweds flat silver in a King Richard pattern and the Temples presented the bride and groom with a silver service set.

After the receiving line Shirley and John, followed by their wedding party, wandered over to the playhouse. Shirley smoked as she walked down the path, and drank champagne openly. Near midnight she and John cut the wedding cake for a phalanx of photographers. Before going upstairs to change, she threw her bouquet to the bridesmaids. Half an hour later she reappeared wearing a dove-grey wool suit with powder blue trim and beret, and the couple ran to the Temple driveway under a shower of rice to a new-looking station-wagon that would take them on their honeymoon of seven days—all that was left of John's furlough.

The Agars' wedding night was spent at the Town House in Los Angeles, and the rest of their honeymoon in Santa Barbara, ninety miles north-west. When they arrived at the Town House at 1.15 am on the 20th a newly-wed army major and his bride who had arrived a few hours before had mistakenly been given the Temple–Agar suite. Embarrassed night clerks obtained another suite, without flowers. 'Anyway, I got the right husband,' Shirley giggled.

Or so it seemed for a while. After John returned to his base, Shirley moved in with George and Gertrude and supervised the refurbishing of her playhouse on the four-acre estate into a honeymoon cottage. 'We'll put up a fence,' Shirley said. 'You'd better,' said her mother, 'we don't want your dogs and kids running over here.' Shirley enrolled in a cooking school. 'At least I'd better know how to cook for John,' she said. 'I want to fix his first supper after we remodel our house. I'll serve him spam and beans; he's got to feel at home.'

Apart from her marriage, Shirley looked and behaved pretty much as any other seventeen-year-old living at home with her parents. She had a dainty but well-rounded figure. She talked in teen vernacular ('super' and 'terrific' were the big words in 1945). She asserted her own strong will and began to resent, albeit mildly, some of the interference by her mother and certain members of the Selznick organisation. She pondered going to college (the University of California at Los Angeles) but decided to continue her studies under private tutors at the Selznick studio.

'I think I'll start by taking Spanish and psychology,' she told a visitor, who then asked, 'Why psychology?' A Selznick press agent interjected, nervously, with: 'That's difficult to answer. Why does anyone want to study psychology? It's like asking, "Why do you like baseball?"' Shirley cut him off: 'It's not anything of the kind,' she snapped. 'I'm interested in psychology because I want to know more about people. I've got to learn the psychology of being a wife anyway.'

All summer before her wedding, when she wasn't preparing for it, she hung around with her friends from school. She even visited Westlake. 'It was fun, walking around like old grads,' she said. She enjoyed dancing in the evening, wore inexpensive girlish clothes at home, played with her pet pekinese and enjoyed the beach at Santa Monica. Shirley was giggly, but not gushy in the Hollywood manner; at the Selznick studios she was everybody's darling as she had been at Fox. But her crowd was never made up of filmland's 'sophisticates' and she never called anyone 'darling'. Her make-up, even for public occasions, was conservative and subdued, especially for the post-war period : no eyeshadow, very little rouge and only a slight amount of lipstick.

Shirley continued her career, and planned to go on working at least until John was discharged and they made decisions about his career and having children. Three weeks after her wedding she was in Denver for a victory bond benefit show appearance. A remake of *Little Women*, with Shirley playing either Beth or Amy, was announced as her first film after her return to the Selznick lot. The picture happened, more than two years later, but without Shirley. Margaret O'Brien played Beth and Elizabeth Taylor, Amy.

In October 1945, a film Shirley had made earlier in the year for Columbia was released : *Kiss And Tell*, based on the hit Broadway play of two years before about three romantic but prankish teenagers and their feuding parents. As Corliss Archer, a famous 1940s teenager Shirley would play once again, she won lavish praise from critics and instant box office success. *Time*'s usually caustic film reviewer called Shirley, as Corliss, 'a first-rate comedienne and a very attractive young lady (who) forgot none of the tricks that once made her the cinema's most dreaded scene thief'.

John returned from the service and he and Shirley moved into their ten-room 'cottage'. He had thought at one time of joining the family meat-packing business in Chicago, but meeting and marrying Shirley had changed all that. While she shunned the glamorous social side of Hollywood, he loved the constant whirl of parties, restaurants and clubs. She still loved her drugstore ice-cream soda fountain, while he preferred drinking something stronger. For the first six months of the marriage, these differences hardly mattered, and the Selznick publicity machine, the columnists, Louella Parsons and Sheilah Graham especially, told the world how happy Shirley and John Agar were.

Shirley's eighteenth birthday party, with John in beaming attendance, was given by RKO on the set of *Honeymoon*, a picture she was filming with Franchot Tone and Guy Madison. Although the film-going public had been pummelled with incidents affirming Shirley's adulthood, from her first long dress and first screen kiss to her marriage, the party was billed as yet another entry into official adulthood. 'Little Miss Marker is burning down the Little Red Schoolhouse and playing legal hookey for the first time,' read the invitation for 23 April 1946, at 4.00 pm. Shirley did burn down a replica of a little red schoolhouse for the 150 guests, who included former co-stars James Dunn, Jack Oakie and Adolphe Menjou. Hamburgers, hot dogs, salad and cokes were served and a band played.

A woman wearing a big placard labelled 'Welfare Worker' and representing Shirley's studio tutors was run off the sound-stage by a man dressed as 'Father Time'. Sailor Vincent, a well-known stuntman and longtime friend of Shirley's, brought in a phoney paste birthday cake while the band played *Happy Birthday*. He tripped in front of her and fell flat on his face in the cake. He then brought in a real cake with eighteen candles, and John helped Shirley blow them out.

In her next film, *The Bachelor and the Bobby Soxer*, filmed in the late summer of 1946, Shirley was scheduled to do some more growing up : taking her first screen drink (anyone who had attended her wedding already knew she was anything but an off-screen abstainer). This so incensed The Women's

Christian Temperance Union's president, Mrs D. Leigh Colvin, that she protested to RKO (who again had Shirley on loan from Selznick, who was deliberately keeping her away from direct competition with Jennifer Jones). Mrs Colvin said Shirley would be 'doing a disservice to American youth if she drank on the screen. Shirley might lure unthinking teenagers to do the same thing.'

Mama Gertrude Temple, RKO's press agents and even Selznick himself were put in a spot over the protest and the studio vigorously denied that Shirley actually drinks in the picture. The script of *The Bachelor and the Bobby Soxer* called for Shirley to develop a crush on an older man, thirty-five-year-old bachelor Cary Grant, so the studio explained to the WCTU. She goes to his apartment in his absence and a boy bellhop lets her in. Trying to be grown-up, the boy offers Shirley a cocktail—equal parts bourbon and scotch. She sips it, makes a face and spurns the cocktail without actually drinking it. Pure situation comedy, said RKO, and the WCTU should be satisfied that Shirley spits out the drink. Besides, Cary Grant doesn't get to debauch the bobbysoxer.

Innocent fun on screen perhaps, but at home Shirley and John were having less and less domestic bliss. Despite flurries of premature rumours to the contrary, the couple didn't have their first child until January 1948. Shirley was nineteen. The baby was named Linda Susan Agar (although almost from the beginning she was called simply Susan) and before she was less than a month old Selznick tried to sign her for films—in fact, he had tried to make the deal even before the child was born. The terms: $100 weekly for the first three years of the baby's life (without working), at which point Selznick would have an option on its services; in the case of twins, $200 a week. In February 1948, Selznick visited the Agars 'to see the baby' but got nowhere. Shirley was determined that her daughter 'Susie' should not be subjected to life as a child star.

The baby at least shored up the public image of the Agar marriage and John himself turned out to be the new prodigy film star. He appeared with Shirley, John Wayne and Henry Fonda in John Ford's *Fort Apache* in 1948, and with her and Robert Young in 1949's *Adventure in Baltimore*. But he had no visible acting talent and naturally his earnings were far less than hers. He got tired of being 'Mr Shirley Temple', a consort to Hollywood's princess. He kept erratic hours and indulged in heavy drinking. They had frequent quarrels. He complained that her life was too ordered and told friends it was difficult to have any fun with Shirley. Because her life was ordered she wanted to stop short of breaking up home and family, but she said John had driven her to the brink of suicide.

Both Shirley and John found solace in other people. Rumours swirled about an odd pentangular relationship among the Agars, singer Johnny Johnston (*Spring Will Be a Little Late This Year*) and his wife, musical film star Kathryn Grayson (*Showboat, Kiss Me Kate*), and Joe Kirkwood Jnr, a professional golfer who also played Joe Palooka on screen. Kirkwood had been a golfing partner of Agar's at the Riviera Country Club in Pacific Palisades, and best man at the Johnston–Grayson wedding. Agar had started to stray when they were a year and a half into the marriage. After a six-day thinking period in Palm Springs, in October 1949, twenty-one-year-old Shirley Temple decided to sue twenty-eight-year-old John Agar for divorce, seeking no reparations but asking custody of Susan, then twenty months old.

She released the news in routine Hollywood style by telephoning columnist Louella Parsons. 'It's not sudden,' Shirley told Louella. 'I didn't want to break up my home and my marriage but there's no other way. I don't want to hurt John. I want our separation and divorce to be dignified. I am merely going to charge cruelty. John is a nice boy, but he's a little

81

mixed up. The worst thing about all this is what it will do to the baby.' To Sheilah Graham, Louella's rival, Shirley said, 'The trouble with my marriage started two and a half years ago, when Johnny started to drink. My suit doesn't mention drinking, but it has become unbearable.'

Agar said he was going home to his mother and announced he was not going to contest the divorce, which Shirley filed only on the grounds of mental cruelty. 'I agree with Shirley that it must be done in a dignified manner,' he said, adding when asked why he wasn't fighting back, 'My shoulders are big enough.'

Hollywood tended to take Shirley's side in the split. She was after all the bigger star, and a likable, friendly and sensible young lady. After ruling that Agar's share of community property be put in trust for Susan, the judge who granted Shirley's decree remarked : 'This plaintiff occupies a place in the hearts and affections of the country, and the failure of her marriage was a distressing disappointment to many people.' This time Shirley really had become an adult publicly, and to ease her distress, the judge restored her maiden name of Shirley Temple.

In later years, Shirley would only say of her first marriage; 'My husband was twenty-four when we married and became an actor after we got married. But this turned out to be a poor decision. I would say that neither one of us was ready for marriage at that time. And so it did not work out. But the one bit of philosophy I learned then—and I still use it— is to give yourself another chance. You've always heard of other people giving you another break. I believe in do-it-yourself too. I was married a second time and it's a magnificent marriage.'

Chapter Seven

Even before the break-up of her marriage, Shirley's career had gone into a rapid decline. While none of her later pictures (in the years 1947–49) actually lost money, she wasn't setting box office records either, and the films had a cheap 'B' look about them and indifferent performances from her. In 1947, when she was nineteen, she made 'my favourite adult picture', *That Hagen Girl* co-starring Ronald Reagan, the future Governor of California and Shirley's later political ally. The story-line was straight soap opera but it did give her a chance to act, and even to attempt to commit suicide—one cruel critic wrote that it was too bad the attempt had failed.

In *The Story of Seabiscuit* Shirley co-starred with a cousin of the famous racehorse. She made *Mister Belvedere Goes to College* with Clifton Webb while—without the studio's knowledge—she was pregnant with Linda Susan. 'We wrote the script of that one as we went along and it was a good idea,' she recalled in half-hearted defence. Her last film was *A Kiss for Corliss* with David Niven in 1949. She recreated her screen character from *Kiss and Tell* but the result, as she admitted, 'was not terribly good'.

Selznick, who still held her contract, suggested, not very gently, that after the divorce Shirley should go to Italy with her daughter and study acting, and even possibly take a different name. She had been type-cast, he said, and her career was going nowhere. As proof of that he told Shirley that he had suggested her for a part in a film to be directed by Carol Reed, who was later to be knighted and to win an Oscar for *Oliver!* Reed had replied sneeringly, and called her a 'little bon-bon with a candy smile' who couldn't act and had no character. Never one to be self-deluded, Shirley admitted that there had been 'none of the pictures in the grown-up period that I'm really proud of', and she quit films once again, and this time for good. She was twenty-one years old.

Her marriage and career absolutely ended, Shirley took off, in January 1950—not for Italy but for Hawaii. She took her daughter and her mother and father by clipper aeroplane and the foursome settled into a rented house near Diamond Head on Oahu, presumably for a two-week stay. Shirley brooded about her life situation, while her old friends in the islands gave a round of parties for the trim and glamorous ex-film star. The guest lists always included a number of single and attractive young men, invited in an effort to cheer her up. Shirley was only half-grateful. 'I didn't like men at all, at that point,' she recalled.

The plot then became even more soapy than some of her films. A tall (compared to her), dark, handsome, rich and socially acceptable young stranger walked into her life. He had skipped two of the parties for Shirley—to go surfing— but Charles Alden Black of San Francisco managed to make it to a third one. 'It's corny,' Shirley recalled, 'but, you know, "Some Enchanted Evening . . . across a crowded room." ' Black further endeared himself to the guest of honour by first mistaking her for a secretary working in Honolulu (normal

American young womanhood at last!) and then admitting that he had never seen a Shirley Temple film.

Black was thirty years old, having been born in Oakland, California on 6 March 1919. He had gone to Hotchkiss, Harvard and the Stanford business school, and his father was James B. Black, president, and later chairman, of Pacific Gas and Electric Company, the largest private utility company in the world. Reputedly one of the richest young men in California, Charles Black had been a naval officer in World War II, was awarded the U.S. Navy's Silver Star, and had twice been cited for bravery in the Pacific. He was in Hawaii in 1950 as assistant to the president of Hawaiian Pineapple.

The instant romance between Charles and Shirley forced her two-week stay to extend to a month and a half, and in tears Shirley finally left Honolulu on 12 March 'sort of engaged'—although her divorce from Agar would not be final until December of that year. Later in March Black resigned from the pineapple company and moved back to San Francisco. In April, Louella Parsons heard of the story, and broke it first on her Sunday radio show, then in her Monday column. Shirley, holidaying with her parents in Del Monte, California, denied that there was any engagement, but she did go up to San Francisco later in April to attend The Bachelor's Ball with Charles Black.

It turned out to be his last Bachelor's Ball, because when her divorce decree became final, Charles and Shirley were married, on 16 December 1950, at his parents' home in Monterey. The whole Black family were avid in their dislike of publicity, never wanting to be photographed, much less interviewed, and Charles was no exception. Thus the press didn't find out about Shirley's second marriage until after her quiet second honeymoon at Cypress Point. (Being married to a former film star had a second disadvantage apart from publicity: Charles was dropped from the Social Register.)

Charles had taken a job with television station KTTV in Los Angeles, and the Blacks and Susan, who was legally adopted by her step-father, moved into a house in Bel-Air. But, in April 1951, Charles was recalled into the Navy as a Lieutenant Commander, and assigned to Washington, D.C. In leaving the Bel-Air house Shirley had to deal with her doll collection, then numbering 740 dolls and insured for $30,000. She decided to lend the collection to the State of California for five years, and they were placed on display at the State Exposition Building in Los Angeles.

There were original Ravca (French) dolls with silk stocking faces and dolls made of dried apples, whose constantly-forming mould had to be cleaned away. The smallest doll was made of porcelain and stood one and a half inches high; the largest was the Japanese bride she had been given in Hawaii. Other dolls represented Gainsborough's 'Blue Boy' and Lawrence's 'Pinky', and various countries of the world: Mexico, Ireland, Germany, and French Indo-China.

A section of the exhibition was devoted to nursery tales: the Old Woman Who Lived in the Shoe, and the Three Little Pigs. Bill Robinson had given his protégée a carved wooden doll in his likeness, complete with a moveable face, a derby hat and the ability to whistle, and it was on display along with dolls representing 'The Spirit of '76'. To round out the exhibition there were several dolls that looked like Shirley Temple.

Crossing the continent by car Charles was forced to leave Shirley and Susan in Tulsa, Oklahoma, because Shirley's appendix had to be removed. She eventually joined him in a cosy apartment on Wyoming Avenue, off Connecticut Avenue in the District, behind an old building in which Vice-President Alben Barkley, among others, had lived. Shirley's near-journalistic curiosity attracted her to a U.S.S.R. office building across the street from the flat; she spent days in rapt but unproductive casing of it.

'I loved Washington,' she recalled. 'It has such a small town air about it. Everyone whispers and looks so important. I was pregnant most of the time, or so it seemed. When I look at pictures of myself at Embassy parties I get bigger and bigger and bigger.' At the suggestion of a top naval officer, Shirley decided to have her baby at Bethesda Naval Hospital to help wartime morale. Charles Alden Black Jnr was born there on 28 April 1952, but complications following the Caesarean section birth briefly threatened Shirley's life. Although her illness was covered by the nation's press, Shirley had caught some of her husband's publicity-shyness: the first photographs of Charles Jnr weren't released until he was seven months old.

The Blacks bought a house on fashionable River Road in Bethesda, Maryland, to escape downtown Washington's summer heat. The house was in a rustic setting with four acres of land. Shirley would borrow her neighbour's tractor and, wearing a scarf like any contemporary housewife, ride it around to survey her holdings—only to have tourists ask her to move out of the way so they could take photographs of Shirley Temple's house. She picked wild flowers for her husband until they discovered his frequent sneezing was from the local ragweed, unknown in his native California. Shirley herself suffered chicken pox in 1952, a severe case, as is often common to those who do not contract the disease until adulthood. (When Susan asked her once what she had missed in her childhood, Shirley replied: 'Darling, only the mumps!' Those came later, too, in 1955—on both sides.)

Louis Parsons, a vice-president of United States Steel, took the Blacks under his wing socially. They attended and gave small dinner parties where Government officials and foreign diplomats discussed the Cold War, Korea, nuclear armaments, the economy, the United Nations and the future of the world, and the Blacks were invited to, and attended, various embassy functions. For Shirley this represented a whole new area of interest, although Charles had long been interested in politics and world affairs. Both, as Republicans, got even more into the Government mainstream after the election of Dwight Eisenhower to the Presidency in November 1952, and his inauguration in January 1953. 'During the two years we were in Washington, I had meant to get involved only in local politics,' Shirley recalled in 1974. 'After all, I was finally old enough to vote. But, of course, in Washington local politics are national and international politics.'

Charles was discharged from the Navy after the Korean War and the Blacks were free to move back to Los Angeles in May 1953. There he worked as business manager of another television station, KABC-TV. On 9 April 1954, Shirley's second daughter and third child, Lori Alden Black, was born at Santa Monica Hospital, where Shirley had also been born. The same nurse who had attended Shirley's birth and later Lindo Susan's was rebooked for Lori's debut, which was also accomplished by Caesarean section.

From time to time Shirley was approached to do television and film work, and even to act on stage, something she'd never done. 'I worked for eighteen years,' she said in declining the offers, 'that's long enough. My only contract is a marriage contract, and my only role is motherhood,' she added. Even Selznick asked her to come back, to do a part in the Thomas A. Edison Centennial television show, and she was tempted. 'I accepted on the telephone,' she remembered, 'and then little Charlie got sick and I called back and said, "I guess I'm too much of a mother". But I would have done it if I had only realised that my father-in-law's company was one of the sponsors.'

In September 1954, Charles became director of business operations for the Stanford University Research Institute, and the Blacks moved once again, to Atherton, twenty-eight miles south of San Francisco. Atherton was an aggressively upwardly mobile, upper middle class area that contained some fancy estates with gates and long drives, and one-acre subdivisions. The Blacks chose a plain beige-coloured, one-storey Californian ranch-style house with five bedrooms on a tree-lined cul-de-sac. Shirley decorated the house herself, and until she undertook a television series in late 1957 also did all the cooking, confining her paid help to a once-a-week cleaning woman. 'My taste is very conservative,' she avowed. 'I'm drawn to Oriental things but I don't think one can have many unless the house is to be all Oriental.'

And so she mixed together her ancient Tibetan scroll, American Oriental furniture and carriage lamps from the gates of the Bethesda house. The entrance hall featured a six feet by two feet bed of pure white pebbles in which sat glass net floats and bottles Shirley and Charles had scavenged from Hawaii's beaches. On a green cement patio at the rear of the house Charles built an L-shaped rock garden with a fountain and a Buddha statue. Shirley planted birds-of-paradise even though she had been told they wouldn't grow in northern California (they did for her) and roses and bamboos off the patio.

Hollywood was represented by the bookcase behind the living-room piano where, in a neat row, reddish-brown leather albums were lined up, with the title of one of Shirley's films lettered in gold on each. The albums contained stills from, and clipping about, the films. (The Blacks also kept a leather album for each year of their marriage, most containing photographs taken by Charles.) And although Shirley swore that none of her children would be subjected to show business until they were adults and chose it for themselves, their bedrooms were full of Shirley Temple touches. In Lori's room there was a screen decorated with pictures of little Shirley, and the Christmas that Lori was three, Santa Claus gave her a Shirley Temple doll. In Charlie's room a photograph of Mom as moppet hung on one wall, and Susan, like her mother before her, had what looked like a doll factory for a bedroom and what most people would consider far too many toys.

Other than indulging their children, the Blacks were not interested in conspicuous consumption, and for independently wealthy people lived way below their means. They owned two cars between them, but both were Chevrolets, one a station-wagon, the other a convertible. Shirley had to work a little harder at being a suburbanite—or 'exurbanite' as she preferred it—than most of the neighbourhood women. But she accomplished it gracefully, and determinedly played the role of the wife next door for a while.

She was active in several charity groups, mostly ones involved in helping children. Although a member of the Peninsula Children's Theatre (which brought low-cost live theatre to young audiences) she was never asked to act by them, even when the group did *Heidi*. 'I guess I'm not the type,' she sighed, 'but I knew something about that one.' So instead she ushered, painted scenery, and served as hospitality and publicity chairman. In the latter capacity she sent identical releases to all the local newspapers; no one printed them. She tried 'exclusives' and one San Francisco paper wrote back asking her please to double space, put her name, address, organisation's name and phone number in the upper left-hand corner, and use fewer than eight carbons.

Every Monday Shirley put on a smock to sell goods at the Allied Arts Guild, which supported a children's convalescent home. She worked for a rehabilitation centre for crippled children and adults. When her brother George developed multiple sclevosis, she went to work for the national organisation to combat the disease.

Charles changed jobs again in 1957 and became director of corporate relations for the Ampex Corporation in nearby Redwood City. He and Shirley went into San Francisco ('the city') only about once every two weeks, but they did see friends in the neighbourhood a few times a week. In 1954 both joined the conservationist Sierra Club and began their long-standing involvement in the problem of ecology. With the children they went on picnics near the ocean, and took to rock hunting. Shirley liked to snorkel and Charles favoured skin diving. Both played golf, with her score ranging from 100 to 125 for eighteen holes. They went to bed and got up early, and once all the kids were at least in nursery school life was, in Shirley's words, 'very quiet and very nice'.

Chapter Eight

Come-backs in any field are tricky, and are therefore usually carefully mulled over and plotted before being attempted. Those in show business involving a change of medium—and dependent on a fickle public—are especially so. After her first come-back in films, starting with some promise and fizzling into a lack of creativity on her part and total indifference on the audience's, Shirley certainly had no desire to try motion pictures ever again. But television (still largely in its 'live' phase in the late 1950s) was still new enough to seem fascinating and challenging. Shirley's children, like most other Americans, adored TV, although their parents strictly controlled their selection of programmes and limited their total viewing time.

The three Black children saw very few films, even their mother's. When Susan saw her first Shirley Temple film, *Rebecca of Sunnybrook Farm*, her five-year-old's critique was, 'Mommy, you didn't sing very well.' Told that her mother as Rebecca was pretending to have lost her voice in that portion of the film, Susan repeated: 'You still didn't sing very well.'

'I used to show my movies to the children when they were little,' Shirley recalled in 1974. 'I thought I had a neat opportunity at their birthday parties. That worked with each child beautifully until about age seven. Then they said, "Can't we go to the roller rink or do something besides seeing one of those old films?" '

Television was a different story. Although she had been consistent in her refusals to consider TV offers from 1950–57 and 'concentrated totally on being a housewife and mother— and of course a born volunteer', the proposal for *Shirley Temple's Storybook* was something else. After all, in her words, 'As a child I lived in a storybook world; it was like living in books instead of just reading them. I *was* Heidi in Switzerland, Wee Willie Winkie in India, the Little Princess in England, and I got to sit on Abraham Lincoln's knee. Imagine a little girl being allowed to dress up in those wonderful Civil War costumes, with pantalettes and hoop skirts! Nothing was impossible and it all seemed real. How can any of us, however grown up, deny the importance of make-believe in our lives?' And she asked 'Aren't all of us living and working for things that we hope will come true?'

Henry Jaffe had been executive producer of Dinah Shore's live television variety show and a producer of *Producer's Showcase*, a well-mounted series of TV spectaculars begun in 1953. He had had particular success in the latter with productions of *Peter Pan* and *Jack and the Beanstalk* and wanted to do a whole series of fairy tales for T.V. Jaffe was accidentally seated next to Shirley Temple Black in March 1957 at a testimonial dinner in his honour given by AFTRA, the radio and television actors' union. Nervous about the occasion, Jaffe had a headache, couldn't eat and could barely speak. He gaspingly requested an aspirin from Shirley. 'I've never been sick a day in my life,' she exaggerated, explaining why she didn't have one. 'I felt terrible,' Jaffe recalled, 'particularly when I had to make a speech. I could hardly stand. But little Shirley helped me up and practically held me there.'

The brief encounter led Jaffe to choose Shirley as the hostess-narrator of his fairy tale series, quickly titled *Shirley Temple's Storybook*. He sent his associate, Alvin Cooperman, to Atherton to see her. 'I told Shirley what we had in mind and she seemed to know immediately how we wanted it done,' Cooperman recalled. 'It was just the kind of show she approved of and we just sat there and talked it over.' To his surprise, Shirley was so sure she wanted to do it—and Charles Snr. had voiced the family's consensus : 'It might be nice'—that 'she got out her typewriter and we worked out a one-page contract. Shirley didn't have an agent and she laughingly suggested maybe she should call her lawyers. But she didn't. When the one page sounded right to her she just sat right down and signed it, on the bridge table in her living room.'

Later the contract was redone by Shirley's lawyers. It grew longer, but didn't contain anything of substance that Shirley hadn't already included in the one-page draft. 'I'm a lawyer,' marvelled Jaffe. 'But if I needed a lawyer, I'd take Shirley.' 'I think it's because Shirley is interested in everything that is going on around her,' added Cooperman. 'So naturally she'd be interested in business too.'

Between the contract signing in April 1957, and the first show's air date, 12 January 1958, Jaffe lined up Sealtest and Hills Brothers Coffee as East Coast and West Coast sponsors, respectively, along with Breck Hair Products for nation-wide sponsorship. Sixteen shows were scheduled, with three to be done live and thirteen recorded. The budget for each live show was an incredibly low $100,000 (versus $400,000–$500,000 for *Producers' Showcase*), with that amount coming from the sponsors. Screen Gems, a subsidiary of Columbia Pictures, did the filming on the other shows and paid any costs over $100,000. The National Broadcasting Company's

TV network took on the additional cost to do the first show in colour. Shirley had script approval and would appear in three shows in an acting role, doing the other thirteen as hostess-narrator (a chore she was told it would be possible to do in one day in Los Angeles out of each month; it actually took three days a month).

Mack David and Jerry Livingstone, who had written the music for Walt Disney's *Cinderella*, wrote *Dreams Are Made For Children*, which Shirley sang to open and close the programme, and the other music for the series. Shirley was worried about how she'd sound since she hadn't sung—except for a bit for RKO that was cut into insignificance in a teen film—since she was eleven. As narrator she appeared in the opening shot of each show in a ball gown by Don Loper (none of the sixteen different ones—one for each show—cost less than $600) on a wool-decked platform designed to resemble a floating cloud, backed by eight chiffon draperies and two chandeliers. She sat on a movable bicycle seat hidden by her dress and anchored on a pole. A large fairy tale book showed scenes from the stories.

Beauty and the Beast was chosen as the opening show because the story could be told on television almost identically to the original written fairy tale already familiar to the viewing audience. Claire Bloom and Charlton Heston, near the beginnings of their careers, were hired to play the title parts, and E. G. Marshall played the merchant. Claire Bloom could hardly wait to meet the narrator and fascinatedly watched Shirley's rehearsals. 'I loved her when I was a little girl,' explained Clare, 'I always called her Shirley Tempa.' Five and a half-year-old Charles Jnr, a little cheekier when he heard the première programme was *Beauty and the Beast*, said, 'Gee, mom, you'll make a nifty beast.'

But Shirley's first acting in the storybook series came in Dutch costume and blonde wig as the flirtatious Katrina Van

Tassel in *The Legend of Sleepy Hollow*. It took ten days to prepare for live telecasting. 'Shirley learned her lines in two days,' Cooperman said, 'and was ready for direction when she came down from Atherton for rehearsals.' Shirley read all the scripts carefully—whether she was going to appear in them or not—and made suggestions for changes. In *Beauty and the Beast* she felt that Beauty did not change character enough as the show progressed. 'So we did quite a lot of rewriting and Shirley was right,' said story editor Norman Lessing.

'I didn't know she was really reading all that stuff,' said Jaffe. 'We sent it to her as a matter of course. But not only did she read all the scripts, she also came up with some good ideas; I don't know whether they were intuitive or the products of her measured thinking, but they were always incisive. She had such good taste and such a sense of fitness of things that we consulted her on many things that didn't concern her.'

Shirley carried out her hostess chores in a slightly babyish sing-song voice, and was a bit glassy-eyed for the small home screens. Jaffe and Cooperman were delighted, however. 'She had all the warmth and laughter in her voice that the series needed,' said Cooperman. 'She was the storyteller telling stories to her children. Nobody could be better.' Jaffe extolled : 'There were unexplored depths in Shirley as an actress, dancer and singer. But to plumb those depths would take time, and Shirley didn't want to be tied up in her new career for more than a few days a month.'

The sixteen shows, which were not shown on a regular night, but rather pre-empted different NBC shows during children's evening viewing hours in 1958, also included *Rumpelstiltskin* live and *The Nightingale, Dick Whittington and His Cat, Hiawatha, Charlotte's Web* and *Son of Aladdin* recorded. *Mother Goose* starring Elsa Lanchester in the title role and with Shirley as Polly Put-the-Kettle-on was the grand

(Above left)
Guy Madison and Shirley clowned
in **Honeymoon**, 1947.

(Below left)
In **Mr Belvedere Goes to College**, in
1948, Shirley took second billing to
Clifton Webb (centre) in the title part.

(Above right)
The all-star cast of **Since you
Went Away**. From left, Claudette
Colbert, Joseph Cotton, Jennifer
Jones, Shirley Temple, Monte
Wooley, Lionel Barrymore,
Robert Walker, in order of
billing.

(Below right)
Shirley co-starred with Ronald
Reagan in 1949's **That Hagen
Girl** and twenty years later, as
Governor of California, he was one
of her political mentors.

(Above)
Charles and Shirley Temple Black were married in 1950.

(Below)
Charles Black turned out to be Mr Right; Shirley met him in Hawaii, recovering from her divorce from John Agar.
(Credit: Harry Redl for Life.)

(Above)
In the 1950s and no longer in the cinema herself, Shirley took a back seat to newcomers like Robert Wagner, here chatting with her at a Hollywood premiere.

(Below)
*In 1957, getting ready to make her television debut, Mrs Black watches herself in 1937's **Rebecca of Sunnybrook Farm**.*
(Credit: Phil Stern for Life.)

(Above and opposite page)
Susan Agar became Susan Black, a high
school graduate and a Northern
California debutante under Mom's
watchful eye.
(Credit: Alfred Eisenstaedt for Life.)

*In 1967 Shirley Temple Black came second in a field of eleven for a seat in the United States Congress from San Mateo County; she ran against three other Republicans pictured here — and lost to Paul ('Pete') McClosky, on her immediate left. (**Credit: Fred Kaplan— Black Star.**)*

*Charles, Shirley and Susan Black arrive
in Ghana, and Madame Ambassador
gives her first press conference at
the airport in Accra, 1974.*

<table>
</table>

(Above)
A game-lover since childhood, Shirley giggles over a chess problem, Woodside, 1974. **(Credit: Baron Wolman for People.)**

(Below)
Mrs Black talks of her Ambassadorship to Ghana just prior to leaving for Accra — to author Robert Windeler — in Woodside, 1974. **(Credit: Baron Wolman for People.)**

Christmas 1958 spectacular show, and provided Susan, Charles Jnr and Lori Black with their first and only professional acting roles.

Shirley had taken each child singly to the filming of one of her shows to be sure each understood the need for her brief monthly absences in Hollywood. And Lori at three and a half had been quite put out at not being allowed to sing on the first *Storybook* show. But Shirley had been determined that her children must not be exploited as professional actors, and none had shown any particular inclination toward acting, singing or dancing. When the family was still in the Washington area, Susan was cast as a fairy in a pre-Christmas school version of *Cinderella*. 'I made her costume out of crepe paper and tinsel ribbon, and built gossamer wings,' Shirley recalled. 'I was amazed to learn that the school was selling tickets to the play in a public auditorium with the promise of Susan's appearance in her stage debut. Off I marched to withdraw her from the school. I have no reason to regret my decision despite the wintry blast of publicity. I was not going to let her appear before four hundred people, nor let anyone commercialise on my daughter's presence.'

Bit parts in *Mother Goose* for national television, under Mommy's watchful eye, were something else again. A stage-hand said the word 'shit' during rehearsals, and Shirley had him fired. 'This is a show for children,' she explained to a dumbfounded cast that included a young Joel Grey as Jack of *Jack and Jill* and a young Rod McKuen as Simple Simon. Even Mrs Temple made a return to stage motherdom on the occasion of her grandchildren's professional debuts, and hovered about the set. The girls did their parts very well, but Charlie as a young chap who climbs a pole as look-out and says, 'Here comes Jack, here comes Jack,' was wooden. The director asked him to repeat his line, which Charlie did with only slightly more animation. He was given a pathetic forced round of applause, led by his proud mother, for his second try.

Priorities were shifted in Shirley's 'third life', in as many decades of show business. Now home and family in Atherton were clearly top priority, and work for the first time was something she merely dabbled in. 'It's funny, having to go to the Beverly Hills Hotel in your own city,' she said, 'to get a good night's sleep before you can get into a work mood.' She also found that in the new career there would be competition; only the strong survived the Nielsen ratings. On the other hand, as a child, 'I was never competitive. I never had to work very hard because there weren't many little girls working.'

Already, during the *Storybook* show phase of her life—at ages twenty-nine and thirty, and with a trim 107 pounds on her five-foot-two frame looking far more attractive than the matronly image she was projecting on screen and off—Shirley was putting distance between herself and 'the little girl'. She ran into another star of her early childhood now making a TV come-back, too, on the soundstages of Screen Gems-Columbia: Rin-Tin-Tin. 'I class myself with Rin-Tin-Tin,' she said at the time. 'In the Depression people were looking for something to cheer them up. They fell in love with a dog —and with a little girl. It won't happen again.'

She refused to draw on the little girl for her *Storybook* work. 'I feel like she's a relative of mine,' said the adult Shirley, 'yet I'm sort of detached and critical.' And on TV she certainly wouldn't be singing any of little Shirley's familiar songs, she told fans and newsmen—least of all, *On The Good Ship Lollipop*. 'I got awfully tired of singing that even as a kid,' she explained. 'I simply was asked to sing it too many times.'

Chapter Nine

'Marriage at its best,' said Shirley Temple Black in her mid-forties, 'should never limit a woman who wants to and must keep growing, continue her education and widen her scope.' For Shirley, ever since she had entered that pre-school race to see who would be the first girl in her class to the altar (and won it, but lost at the same time), 'it was very important to have a husband'. On the other hand, she had begun working for a living when she was three and had established an indelible separate identity through that work; being Shirley Temple was quite independent of who her husband was. Indeed, it didn't matter whether or not she had a husband at all—to the public, that is. To her, it mattered a lot.

Fortunately, in Charles Black Shirley had 'the kind of husband who pushes me out the door. He likes me to get involved. He urges me on. But he also lets me make my own decisions.' Charles and Shirley had mutual and long-standing interests in ecology and the law of the sea. And, especially after he founded and became president of the Mardela Corporation, which was involved in marine instrument resource development, 'acquaculture'—methods to get food from the seas, fish, algae and seaweed—and she became involved in the United Nations, Charles and Shirley's working lives paralleled. 'We've always been on the same track,' she explained, 'that's why we have such a good marriage.'

While Charles certainly encouraged her to get involved in politics, international affairs and diplomacy, Shirley was strong-willed enough to want to make her own way. And, in the fifteen years from 1960, when she was still a show business bubblehead, to 1975 when she was recognised throughout the world as a serious, hard working United States Ambassador to Ghana, she did just that.

There were two further forays into television after the March 1961 filming of the last *Shirley Temple Storybook*, which was shown later that year. In April 1963, Shirley arrived at CBS Television City in Hollywood to tape an hour-long segment of *The Red Skelton Show*. It wasn't yet another come-back, she insisted, but she hinted at some future show business plans and said, 'Fortunately, I can work when I want to.' During the approximately forty minutes of the show in which she was involved, Shirley sang *By the Beautiful Sea* and a few bars of *Side By Side* with Skelton, and in a 'Freddy the Freeloader' sketch entitled 'Passion in Pasadena' she played a very rich girl.

Her star-power was still such that a steady stream of performers from other productions, CBS executives, studio workers and their children trooped through the Skelton set the four days Shirley was working, to meet her and get her autograph. It was highly unusual; most other stars were treated in a more blasé fashion. The show's crew found her, as all her other crews before had, highly professional, un-affected and coolly friendly. The show's choreographer noted that 'all the dancers liked her—and this can be unusual for dancers. She was a star from the time they made real stars.' The crew noticed that Skelton held back his usual ribald antics during Shirley's appearance because she seemed so poised and ladylike. 'I don't think he was uncomfortable,' recalled one stage hand, 'but he certainly didn't act like he did when Martha Raye was here.'

Shirley's rehearsals started on a Saturday, with the actual taping to take place the following Tuesday April 23, her thirty-fifth birthday. She had celebrated with Charles and the children at home in Woodside—where they had moved from nearby Atherton in 1961—before her arrival in Hollywood, where she spent four nights alone at the Sheraton-West, even having her dinner in her room. 'I never saw old friends when I went to Hollywood to work,' she said.

Shirley was a little stiff during rehearsals, but on taping day, her birthday, she loosened up into some Skelton-style clowning. A long loaf of French bread was used in the sketch, and for two days Red had been chewing on it between rehearsals. During a scene in which Shirley got married to the other man and Skelton was supposed to be in tears, she whipped a half loaf of the bread out from under her wedding gown and started munching, breaking him up into laughter.

A reminiscent birthday cake, large enough to feed over a hundred, was wheeled on to the set for Shirley's party. She recalled that she could be only thirty-four if she wanted to, thanks to her parents and Twentieth Century-Fox. 'Fox even produced a phony birth certificate, which I still have,' she said. 'It was quite a shock to be told at what I thought was my twelfth birthday, that I was actually thirteen. I hadn't prepared to be a teenager.' Charles, Susan, Charles Jnr and Lori all sent telegrams on Mom's thirty-fifth, but 'I never did get supper on my birthday because I took the hour break during taping to fix my make-up and hair. I ended up by eating two bananas in my hotel room by myself at ten o'clock that night.' The show must go on.

At the turn of the new year 1965, a show was tailored

just for Shirley Temple. It was filmed at her old studio, Twentieth Century-Fox, which was rapidly becoming more of a production centre for television shows than for motion pictures. The name of Shirley's TV show was *Go Fight City Hall*, and it was a half-hour pilot for the American Broadcasting Company television network, a situation comedy about a young social worker. Shirley was supposed to work for the Department of Public Assistance and play a do-gooder who kept getting into trouble. Her co-stars were Bill Hayes and Jack Kruschen. Had it been successful, the full series of shows would have gone into production in May 1965, and Shirley was promised she could finish her work by September.

She was still insisting that the role she was best suited for was 'wife and mother' and that she had had to get the consent of her husband and all her children to undertake the project. After Susan graduated from high school in June the plan was to take a house on the ocean in Santa Monica or Malibu for the summer, for Shirley and the children. To make the pilot she once again commuted from Woodside. Shirley said on embarking on the series, that she felt there was a great need for social workers, and 'I'm hopeful that the show will create strong interest among young people, particularly women, to go into this line of work'. It never had a chance to, as the network, after seeing the pilot, refused to buy the full series. Ten years later Shirley said, 'I really didn't like the idea; I'm glad it never got off the ground.'

Still, the pilot itself was an event in the Hollywood tradition. 'Welcome Home, Shirley' proclaimed a huge banner furled across the Twentieth Century-Fox studio gate. And there was a champagne lunch in the commissary with old friends and studio executives. Still a resident schoolteacher on the lot, Shirley's tutor, Frances Klampt, 'Klammie', was at the lunch. Shirley recalled that she had celebrated several birthdays in this studio commissary, and that when she had left Fox aged twelve she had left all her baby teeth behind. 'My very nice bungalow is now the studio hospital,' she noted. 'I don't know if there's a message in that or not. If I had kept digging in the ground behind the bungalow I might have struck oil before Fox did.'

Commuting the four hundred miles from the peninsula south of San Francisco to Hollywood for a few days was one thing, but 'children should be older before a woman starts a career in public life', Shirley said in 1974 by way of explaining why she hadn't plunged into politics before her race for Congress in 1967. She had been actively interested in the Republican Party since her Washington years of the early 1950s, and one of the last things Shirley had done before returning to California in 1953 was to meet the new Vice-President of the United States, a fellow Californian and former Senator, Richard M. Nixon. It wasn't until the 1960 Presidential election, however, that she became actively involved. As a volunteer, Shirley was precinct captain for Nixon in his race against John F. Kennedy, and with hundreds of other Republican women of San Mateo County she worked stuffing envelopes, walking precincts, and getting out the vote. Nixon won the county and California, but lost the election. Shirley wasn't discouraged, even after Lyndon Johnson defeated Barry Goldwater in 1964.

She began to accept fund-raising rallies and speaking engagements on behalf of the party, many of them out of state. At the Texas Republican party's state central committee meeting in Houston in early 1967, she talked of 'all of us ordinary citizens getting involved.'

'I so believed that speech,' she said, 'that I decided to run for Congress when it looked like Representative J. Arthur Younger would be too ill to run again.' Younger, a Republican who had represented the generally conservative San Mateo

103

11th Congressional district for twelve years, died suddenly in June. The previous Easter Sunday he had encouraged Shirley to make the race, saying 'I won't be around forever'. 'We didn't know he was as ill as he was,' Shirley recalled. But she took Younger's imprimatur—and the advice of former co-stars George Murphy (*Little Miss Broadway*) and Ronald Reagan (*That Hagen Girl*), who by then were, respectively, the Republican Senator from, and Governor of California—and declared for Congress.

'Little Shirley Temple is not running for anything,' she told a press conference in the Polynesian-style private dining room of Villa Chartier, a San Mateo motel restaurant on 29 August 1967. 'If some one insists on pinning me with a label make it read Shirley Temple Black, Republican independent.' Reagan had set the special off-year election to fill the vacant seat for 14 November, making Shirley's entry dangerously late. She joined a previously listed male field of eleven candidates: three other Republicans and eight Democrats. If none of the twelve achieved a majority vote, a run-off would be held between the top Republican and the top Democrat a month later (although all candidates were listed without party identification on the original ballot).

In an atmosphere more conducive to a Junior League brunch, Shirley, wearing a boxy apricot-coloured suit with a long car coat and jade necklace, explained to the press and a cheering crowd of her own supporters why she, a thirty-nine-year-old housewife and ex-film star, should be sent to Congress. She faced the battery of still and television cameras like the pro that she was, dimpled frequently and demanded to be taken seriously. She attacked President Lyndon B. Johnson for having 'played politics with the Vietnam war and with the riots', and she reached back to her youth for the most crushing of metaphors: 'The Great Society, a pretty bad movie in the first place, has become a Great Flop,' she said.

Shirley said she wanted to do her share 'to help solve some of the critical problems which face the nation today and get the country back on the road to progress. It is not progress for the largest, strongest military power in the world to be mired down in an apparently endless war with one of the smallest and weakest countries in the world. It is not progress when some of our citizens participate in bloody riots and burn down whole sections of cities. It is not progress when pornography becomes big business and when our children are exposed to it. It is not progress when some of our young people are so uninspired by our present leadership that they reject society, turn to drugs and become so-called "hippies".'

Three attractive peninsula matrons, Shirley's colleagues for thirteen years of charity work, passed out copies of her statement and led a group of mothers and daughters in cheering and applause so excitedly that one member of the press got to the floor and said, 'This is no rally, this is a press conference. Who are these people anyway?' 'I don't know,' smiled Shirley, 'but I'm awfully glad to see them here.' Another questioner wanted to know if she was a dove on Vietnam, given her statement. 'I'm a mother with a fifteen-year-old son, but we do have to honour our commitment there,' she hedged, 'to prevent Communism from taking over. But the job has to be done quickly and LBJ should rely on the Joint Chiefs of Staff for his military advice rather than on McNamar; I don't know what should be done militarily, I'm not a military man.'

As the third former film star to seek office as a California Republican in the last three years, Shirley was asked if she thought actors without political experience were justified in seeking national political careers. 'Not all movie actors should be in politics,' she agreed. 'But then, all haberdashers shouldn't be in politics either,' she added, recalling Harry Truman. And as for Congress specifically, 'no one is experienced in Congress until he gets there', she said. Her qualifications were that she was 'an honest, hard-working woman who will do an honest job. I have lived here over thirteen years; people know what I've been doing since I was three.' Charles, whose father had become a member of Reagan's Committee on Efficiency in Government, was standing at the back of the room. He said that if Shirley won the special election the whole family would go with her to Washington, D.C.

Shirley's position on virtually all issues of the day was vague and waffling. On the civil riots then seemingly sweeping America, mostly in black ghettos, she said, 'We have to stop thinking of each other as being of different colour—we are all Americans. We must have real equality in this country, and the responsibility that goes with it. I'm for anything that will make life better for all Americans. But these people, the Negroes, have been let down. Tremendous promises have been made by the Administration. I feel we need more vocational education and we need to give people suffering in riot areas a sense of meaningful achievement.'

The Congressional campaign itself was like no other in American history. 'Shirley You Jest' read a popular bumper sticker for Republicans and Democrats alike. But Shirley Black wasn't jesting. 'No one really asked me any questions,' she recalled of the 1967 race in 1974. 'During that campaign Vietnam was just about the only thing discussed. They didn't ask me how I felt about the People's Republic of China, which I was even then, in my way, trying to get into the United Nations. They didn't ask me about lowering the voting age to eighteen, about which I had spoken all over the country. But I wasn't asked questions that really said what I was.'

Although a campaign aide conceded that either Shirley or Charles could have written out a cheque for the entire cost of her campaign, Shirley insisted on raising the money in more usual political style, by contributions from other organisations and individuals. But by entering so late, long after the other serious candidates had their financing, she was prevented from conducting the kind of campaign at which she clearly would have excelled: television 'messages'. As it was, she could manage only two thirty-second spots and one one-minute spot, because to reach the small San Mateo constituency it was necessary to buy commercials for the entire San Francisco Bay area, most of whose voters couldn't vote for her. Shirley was offered free exposure on the ninety-minute Jim Dunbar television show before the election, but a strike was on at the station and she wouldn't cross the picket line. 'I have never crossed a picket line in my life and I wasn't about to start then. I would do it again today,' she said in 1974. 'I still wouldn't cross the picket line. But even at that, if the campaign had been two weeks longer I could have won.'

She was forced, therefore, in 'the very clever political campaign against me', to rely on more intimate techniques, such as standing outside factories shaking hands, and meeting men and women at small gatherings 'where they would decide as couples'. Razzle-dazzle entered into the race, and Democrat Roy Archibald, a San Mateo city councillor and former mayor used his World War II PT-boat skipper experience (like President Kennedy's) to give his campaign the image: 'PT-453 versus The Good Ship Lollipop.'

A formal debate requested by one of the other Democrats to make his campaign stand out—the format was popular from the Nixon-Kennedy race and Shirley was thought to be the logical opponent to use to get attention—was held at the El Camino High School gymnasium, shortly before the election. Three other Democrats were included, at Shirley's insistence, but she was the only Republican. 'I am only concerned at conserving party unity,' she said with a wicked grin when asked why she had not invited the others to attend. The evening was clearly orchestrated as a showcase for Shirley.

Wearing a red suit and an overabundance of lipstick, she

arrived on Charles's arm. Her supporters were already there in full force, dancing about in red, white and blue sashes and carrying signs showing a matronly portrait of their candidate. Red balloons with Shirley's picture on them were handed out; a few were popped by little boys supporting one of the other candidates. The four Democrats got only a smattering of applause, while Shirley was wildly cheered as she settled herself on the right-hand side of the podium, under 'HOME' on the basketball scoreboard. The four Democrats huddled on the left, and the referee announced that he was 'the only neutral person they could find—I'm from Berkeley' (outside the district).

Shirley started off with a fifteen-minute speech; each Democrat was allowed ten minutes. Then Shirley replied, followed by each Democrat. Three local newsmen filed on stage and asked questions—almost all of Shirley—and the candidates were allowed a brief reply to the questions. Candidates were not allowed to ask questions of each other and no one from the thousand people in the audience was supposed to speak.

After her opening spiel about coming out of private life to represent 'the forgotten decent people of the country', Shirley made a remark that stunned even her own supporters. 'How can you say "stop the bombing of North Vietnam" when you can make a case that it hasn't even started?' she asked. After an uproar in the hall, she went on to advocate 'a swift and honourable conclusion' to the war. One Democrat, Edward Keating, who followed her said that Mrs Black was 'more to be pitied than censored' and that he and she lived in two different worlds if she thought the bombing had scarcely begun. Another, Andrew Baldwin, called Shirley 'not a dove, not a hawk, but a blackbird'. Archibald warned of escalation and counter-escalation and World War III.

Dan Monaco, who had organised the 'debate' thanked Mrs

Black for being allowed to be present at her meeting; Shirley smiled tightly. She tried to recoup in the question period by saying that she was not, after all, for increased bombing nor for escalation of the war. She was for, naturally, freedom, justice, dignity, honour, friendship and a return to honesty and integrity in government. But it was too late. The voters of her affluent, highly educated district saw through her shallow preparations for public office, and while she had thousands of fans in San Mateo County less than twenty-seven per cent of the electorate wanted her to represent them in Congress.

Ironically, it was none of the Democrats, but a fellow Republican independent, Paul ('Pete') McClosky, who beat her in the special election, largely on the basis of his dove-of-peace stand on the Vietnam War. He went on to represent the district for several more full terms, and in 1972 ran in some Republican primaries for President against Nixon, on an anti-war platform. 'I'm most proud that I came in second out of twelve,' Shirley said in 1974. 'But I wish I could have represented the people of San Mateo county. I think it might have been better for them.'

Chapter Ten

In the Presidential election of 1968 Shirley repressed her disappointment at her own defeat in the Congressional race and heavily involved herself in the national Republican campaign. Even before the candidates, Richard Nixon and Spiro Agnew, were selected she made two hundred speeches around the United States, co-ordinated by the Republican National Committee; she visited forty-six cities in twenty-two states. After the convention picked the Nixon-Agnew ticket, Shirley headed an effort to organise American voters living abroad and herself barnstormed nine foreign countries on behalf of Nixon.

'It was a non-partisan vote drive,' she explained in 1974, 'but obviously we concentrated on likely Republicans. I got the idea from Clare Booth Luce; anyone can do it, it's just whoever thinks of it first.' Absentee ballots from abroad went heavily for Nixon-Agnew, who just managed to squeak by at home, and Shirley had established herself as an appealing vote-getter, at least for other Republicans. Her speeches raised more than $1 million. And her reward was not long in coming. In 1969 Nixon appointed Shirley Temple Black a

United States delegate to the United Nations, for the international organisation's twenty-fourth General Assembly.

There was ample precedent for an entertainer in the U.S. delegation to the U.N. (Marian Anderson, Irene Dunne and Myrna Loy had preceded Shirley in the post), which made her limited international experience slightly less offensive to critics. She had been co-founder, and was currently international chairman of volunteers for, the International Federation of Multiple Sclerosis Societies. 'I call the Federation my little U.N.,' she explained, 'and our secretariat is in Vienna.' In 1969, nineteen countries with multiple sclerosis organisations were members, in 1975 it was twenty-two.

It was on a European trip to set up branches of the Federation—and incidentally to stump for Nixon—that Shirley had found herself besieged in a hotel room in Prague on the day, 20 August, 1968, that Soviet troops took over Czechoslovakia. Fearing arrest, imprisonment or the firing squad Shirley tore a picture of deposed Czech president Alexander Dubcek into bits and flushed it down the toilet. She, along with four hundred other Americans, was later allowed to leave the country by car. 'I think of this occurrence every year on the 20th August,' she recalled more than six years later. 'It was on the 20th August 1974, that President Ford named me Ambassador to Ghana.'

When she arrived in New York in September 1969 to take her seat at the U.N. as the only woman on the five-person American delegation, Shirley carried a vivid red patent leather briefcase decorated with a blue 'N' for Nixon—a souvenir of the victorious election the year before. Many of her countrymen, in and out of the U.N., greeted her appointment with smiles and snickers of derision and disbelief. Delegates and workers at the U.N. from other countries sought her out to get her autograph—'but I asked for all of theirs back', she recalled. 'Everybody at the U.N. is a celebrity for about three days, but then you have to see who gets down to work. The delegates are about the best their countries can send, especially from Africa. They are so well-educated and so young—but they have to be, their countries are.'

The slightly cool and distant receiving-line smile she began to develop as a child greeting prominent visitors to Twentieth Century-Fox served Shirley well at the endless round of U.N. embassy cocktail parties, and she quickly became a popular figure. Threatening letters from a man who said he would kill her forced her to have a bodyguard (a New York City Police detective paid for by the U.N.) with her at all times in New York—but even a bodyguard was something she had once been used to. Shirley lived alone in a luxury suite at the Barclay Hotel; the thirteen weeks of the General Assembly session, despite Charles' several visits and her frequent week-end flights to Woodside, represented the longest stretch of time she had lived apart from any of her families.

One night in the suite, as she was writing a letter to Charles, a creature she took to be a mouse brushed up against her leg. Shirley called the hotel operator and said, 'There's a black mouse in my room.' The operator answered : 'There are no black mice in the hotel—it must be a rat.' And a hotel employee with a flashlight arrived in time to see the rat run off into his hole. Shirley resumed writing her letter, adding a P.S. : 'When you come here bring one of the large—not the small—traps from the cellar.' Charles arrived in due course with not one but two traps. That night they heard the right kind of snap, and Shirley threw the rat's body into the hotel corridor.

Shirley was like no other United Nations delegate had been before or since. For one thing, there was always a group of her fans in the visitors' galleries less interested in the course of international debate than in seeing a former film star. She'd sometimes flash the V-sign at her younger admirers. For another thing, although she understood it, she didn't speak and write in the peculiarly obfuscating jargon of the international bureaucracy. She had a language of her own. 'Yummy' was still one of her favourite words. She used colourful metaphors ('As my Holland ancestors have said, there are two flood tides beating up against the dikes'), and phrases from contemporary pop-sociology : 'social alienation', 'criminal depravity', 'colonial exploitation', 'philosophical umbrellas'.

A delegate from India asked the United States to clarify two technical points, one on national sovereignty and one on airborne sensing techniques pertaining to outer space. Shirley, as the senior U.S. representative present, replied : 'Earlier this year I had the honour to serve on the Citizens' Group of the United Nations Task Force. We know that our planet is an earth spaceship, and all of us are on it together. My delegation feels that through the peaceful use of space we shall be able to achieve peace on our spaceship.' The Indian delegate retorted : 'After hearing the stirring appeal of the representative of the United States, I think I am more confused than ever.'

'I always wrote my own speeches,' Shirley recalled, 'although I had to get them cleared at the U.S. Mission. I went a little too far when I talked about the refugee problem in the Middle East. I compared the problem there to the way America had treated the American Indians. The Indians were our first refugees. I expressed my feelings very colourfully, but the Mission felt it was too harsh. They asked me to soften it, which I did.'

Shirley never felt that her skimpy formal education was a detriment to her career at the United Nations or subsequently. John Ford had named her 'One-Take Temple' because of her ability as a child to get things right the first time. And at the U.N. Charles W. Yost, the head of the U.S. delegation, assigned her to thirteen committees when the normal load was four because she was able to absorb reams of documents and keep up. Yost's basic advice to her was: 'Just be yourself.' 'I'm a fast learner and interested in a lot of things,' she said. 'We all grow. Hopefully one doesn't grow wider necessarily, but more in the brain department. I've had a unique opportunity my whole life to learn. I was studying Mandarin Chinese for six months at age eight, for a movie called *Stowaway*. I can still say a few key works, like "very good".'

The Mainland Chinese hadn't yet arrived during Shirley's U.N. term, though she continued to push for their entry, but there were delegates from more than one hundred other countries ready to pronounce her performance in the thirteen-week General Assembly run 'very good'. 'People were eager to discount her as a dilettante and featherbrain,' said one U.N. expert, 'but she proved them wrong. She took the job very seriously, did her homework and really worked—and before long was highly regarded by almost everybody there.' Saudi Arabian Ambassador Jamil Baroody called Shirley 'a fresh breeze that has gently blown into our midst'. A fellow U.S. delegate noted that 'Shirley is the only one of us who is always on time for appointments.' And Mrs Victoire Golengo of Congo (Brazzaville) found Shirley 'a very pleasant person who takes everything very easily. Even when her government is criticised she doesn't get excited.'

Unflappable and almost always smiling, Shirley was in her forty-first year when at the U.N., plumpish and given to brightly coloured dresses, especially Puccis. Her hemlines—in the age of the mini-skirt—stayed below her chubby knees. She was paid at the rate of $38,000 a year, but only for the three months of the General Assembly session. She turned down a delegate from Morocco and a delegate from Greece who wanted to organise a showing of old Shirley Temple films at the U.S. Mission or at the U.N. itself 'because I thought my motives might be misunderstood'.

U.N. Delegate Shirley Temple Black's typical day began at 6.30 am, the hour she used to get up when at the height of her film career. Exercises to keep trim and help keep her weight down were done on the floor. 'I know all the exercises, I've been doing them forever, I think.' She cooked her own breakfast in the suite's small kitchen, met her bodyguard in the lobby and went by limousine to the U.S. Mission, arriving by 8.45 am. She attended committee meetings, ate official lunches and spent most evenings at diplomatic receptions. On rare nights off she cooked soup in the suite and studied her work for the next day. One of Charles' visits to Shirley in New York was for the weekend of the United Nations Ball at the Grand Ballroom of the Hotel Waldorf-Astoria where, like some younger version of Arthur and Kathryn Murray, they dipped and swooped through 1940s- and 1950s-style foxtrots and rhumbas.

At a dinner given by the Jordanian delegation, Shirley choked on a pine nut from a 'yummy' rice dish that had lodged in her throat. 'I started to black out,' she remembered. 'But then I thought to myself "I'm a representative of the United States and I'm the only one here, and I can't die. If I do, nobody will believe that somebody didn't do something to me on purpose." Finally the nut went down.' Sitting across from the head of the Soviet Mission to the U.N., Yakov Malik, she then 'presented to him what I call "my jovial idea". I suggested that there be only women on the Security Council.' Malik never replied to the suggestion.

Shirley's committee assignments included refugees, social progress, the aging, and the peaceful uses of outer space, but her 'two favourites' were the committees on youth and the environment, 'which suddenly came together, because the youth of this country got extremely interested in environmental problems'. Her maiden speech at the U.N. was the object of a barrage of critical letters because she had urged that the age of majority be lowered from twenty-one to eighteen, a theme left over from her 1967 campaign.

'I think we could stop a lot of the protesting if eighteen-year-olds could do the same things adults do,' she said. 'They would feel more like participants in our society if they had the right to vote, paid taxes and were able to marry without parental consent. The youth of today are a very special generation. I admire them greatly. They're better educated and better informed, and when they protest they're calling us, and I think we have to listen a little better.'

In her official U.N. biographical sketch Shirley listed her profession as 'former actress'. She said, while acknowledging that her fame helped her get attention and get things done, 'Fame is fleeting and it's very sad for people to wallow in the past. The happiest moment is now.' She got along with delegates from 'all countries except two which would not talk to me—Albania and Cuba—because I am American'. In front of the U.S. Mission one day some Black Panthers were agitating. 'I'm not afraid to extend my hand to anybody,' she said, 'although sometimes it hangs there for a long time. So I put my hand out and said, "Hello, I'm Shirley Temple Black." And the fellow said, "Hello, I am a Black Panther." And the very brutal looking man got tears in his eyes and said "Oh, I remember." '

When her U.N. term was up, just before Christmas 1969, Shirley was frustrated by all the work undone. 'The term should be two years,' she said. (Nixon, of course, could have appointed her again, but didn't.) Shirley had made a particular effort to understand and get to know the representatives of the developing nations of the unaligned Third World, and she was particularly popular with them. On the last day of the twenty-fourth U.N. General Assembly, one of her special friends, Angie Brooks from Liberia, was elected President of the General Assembly for the next session. While women from

Third World countries often outnumbered the men and lead delegations, Shirley had occupied the token U.S. 'woman's seat' at the U.N. and showed no predisposition to broaden the role of her sex in international diplomacy.

In fact, at a Republican fund-raising dinner in Philadelphia in October 1970, Shirley, who had become deputy chairman of the U.S. delegation to the U.N. Conference on Human Development, denounced one human development of the day. 'I don't care for Women's Lib—I prefer the strong arms of my husband around me,' she said. In 1974 she agreed that women had 'the right to equal pay, equal opportunity and equal education', but reiterated that she was 'not too fond of some of the methods which have been used to achieve those goals, like bra burning. I was liberated when I was three, I did get equal everything.'

Shirley did acknowledge that she had occasionally been discriminated against at international gatherings where she was the only woman. 'I have been asked to get coffee and sandwiches for the men. I did it at first but I solved the problem by bringing my own coffee with me to work. So I had my coffee when the rest of the group convened and it wasn't that easy for them to send me out, and pretty soon they were bringing in things for everybody, like cookies. I solved the problem by being subtle because the best thing about being a woman is being feminine. That is where we can contribute so much, because we have a different viewpoint.'

At a dinner party in an ambassador's home in another country she wouldn't name for fear of embarrassing it, Shirley had another problem. 'I was the only woman at the dinner party and there were thirteen other countries there. After dinner, when the men went into the other room for brandy and cigars I didn't know what to do. I joined them for a few minutes, then asked the ambassador if his wife was there. She was upstairs and I joined her there.'

Despite her failure to be reappointed to the U.S. delegation to the U.N., Shirley left salaried U.N. work as she had entered it: a total believer in the organisation. 'We would have to invent the U.N. if we did not have it, which is not an original thought,' she said. 'The U.N. acts as the world's conscience, and over eighty-five per cent of the work that is done by the United Nations is in the social, economic, educational and cultural fields. That doesn't make headlines like the Security Council when someone is fighting. These good works are done by U.N. people around the world, but most of the funds and most of the energy is voluntarily contributed.'

Shirley herself became a U.N. volunteer in 1970, visiting countries as varied as Iran, Rumania and Egypt to make speeches about pollution and endangered species. Later in the year she was appointed by Secretary of State William Rogers to be deputy chairman of the U.S. delegation to the Conference on Human Environment, which took place in Stockholm two years later. (Christian Herter Jnr was chairman.) She was paid a per diem allowance of $25 and found herself the only woman out of four hundred men at a preparatory meeting in Stockholm in 1971. That year she was also one of the few women invited to a Nixon White House dinner celebrating the twenty-fifth anniversary of the signing of the United Nations Charter, after the protests over the original plan to make it a stag affair. She used the occasion to ask the administration to submit the Indo-China war to the U.N. Security Council for settlement, although she had previously supported Nixon's handling of the war.

The two-week Stockholm Conference itself, in June 1972, was attended by business leaders and diplomats from 114 countries—only nine of them represented by any women, however—and was, in Shirley's words, 'the most successful world meeting that was ever held—so meaningful that it will be four or five years until the world is really aware of it. We took action on 109 different topics (including endangered species of fur-bearing animals) and drew up a declaration of the human environment, providing guidelines to improving the quality of human existence and insuring human dignity. It has to be an international solution because the air just sweeps around the world without a passport, not respecting boundaries, in about ten days, dropping pollution everywhere. Ocean and river pollution are also international.'

Shirley's speech to the final session of the conference—written with only an hour and half's notice—urging 'the acknowledgement of our kinship as human beings and working together for the rational management of our common resources' won very good notices. It was printed in a paper that came out of the conference and widely reprinted around the world, along with the texts of speeches by Indira Ghandi, Barbara Ward and Margaret Mead.

As an international celebrity Shirley got to meet Yugoslavia's President Tito in Brioni, Yugoslavia; and a Malaysian merchant told her, 'You were my first crush,' in a Moscow restaurant, during her work with the American-Soviet Joint Committee in the Field of Environmental Protection. She addressed members of the same group in Washington on the subject of whales, the largest endangered species of mammals, trying to persuade the Russians to give up whaling as the U.S. had already done. Appropriately in San Francisco—'my home is on the San Andreas Fault'—Shirley announced on behalf of the U.N. to 170 earthquake experts that a worldwide natural disaster 'early warning system' was in the planning stages. The system, designed to provide warning against earthquakes, volcanic eruptions, floods, tidal waves and typhoons, would require every country on earth to participate.

Back in Washington, Shirley made a film for the first time in twenty-four years. She narrated a twenty-minute film about a barber of Honduras who became one of the Western Hemisphere's most admired primitive painters, José Antonio Velasquez, for the Visual Aids Division of the Organisation of American States in the Pan American Union. It was one of a series of OAS films for which film stars provided the voice-over narration without appearing on camera. Shirley was selected for Velasquez because his story was presented 'like a tale for children'. Her travels to many parts of the globe got her into 'the darndest situations sometimes, because on TV and in some movie houses around the world I'm still a little girl. It confuses people, I suppose.'

It was little wonder then, that she found her next full-time assignment somewhat less appealing. In late 1972 Shirley was appointed to the President's Council on Environmental Quality (CEQ), where she seemed to specialise in 'sewage and sludge' in her homeland. A more typical field trip in that post was a five-hour canoe ride through Four Holes Swamp, a black water sanctuary in South Carolina with virgin cypress and 'very good water, full of nutrients. Also full of alligators, cotton mouths.' She resigned quietly from CEQ in January 1974 to plot a return to international affairs.

Chapter Eleven

One reason that Shirley felt comfortable about volunteering for work that took her travelling, and so often abroad, was that her three children had grown up without causing major problems for their parents or themselves. Susan, Charles Jnr and Lori all might be a little square and dull by many of their contemporaries' standards, but at least they weren't hooked on drugs or alcohol like some offspring of famous parents. Nor were they talentless chips trying to launch careers off the old show business block, like other children of Hollywood. 'Except for minor traffic offences,' said Shirley, 'we've had no trouble.'

Susan graduated from Stanford University with a degree in art history, painted for pleasure and wrote a play and several drafts of a novel—both unpublished. Charles earned an undergraduate degree in political science and planned to be an international lawyer specialising in the law of the sea, a strong interest of both his mother and father. Lori, in her mother's words, 'plays the piano very well, is also good with animals—has even gotten into the tank with killer whales, and has always majored in boys'.

At ages twenty-seven, twenty-three and twenty-one in 1975, the three had had extremely conventional and conservative Northern California social lives, more in the tradition of the Blacks than of the Temples. Charles Jnr's longish hair and moustache were as much rebellion as they ever evidenced. 'I raised them pretty much as I was raised,' Shirley explained. 'We have wide open communication—that is very important. No matter what they tell you, you must not be visibly shocked. And you must teach them that they need a sense of humour to survive.'

In Woodside the Blacks held a 'family council every night', rotating the leadership of the discussion. 'We discuss *everything*,' Shirley said, 'politics, what they are doing, what Charles and I are doing. After about age sixteen it is their own direction that they go in, however. Children are sort of on loan to you, you have the pleasure of having them. You don't have that long a time to make your point with your children, and when they are older there is not much more you can give them, except to be available and to keep the door open.' Susan, in the summer of 1975, announced her engagement to Robert Falaschi, the First Secretary of the Italian Embassy in Accra and married him that October, thus becoming the first of the three to leave the nest.

One thing about which Shirley almost never wanted to talk, with the children or anyone else, was finances. 'I just don't feel it's very feminine to talk about money,' she explained, although she did not feel it was unfeminine to make it. 'I don't think it's good taste to talk about it, either.' Shirley was a fiscal conservative at home as well as in her politics ('let's say I'm careful'), which came from having a banker for a father 'and growing up in those Depression years. My earnings have been greatly exaggerated by the press, although I can assure you that I will never be hungry or poor or not be able to take care of my share of the children's future.'

Two matters relating to finances that really galled Shirley were : (1) the fact that she worked on straight salary for the studios—albeit high salaries for the times—and therefore had no financial participation in any re-releases of her films, to television or otherwise; and (2) the accusation that she had bought political position and prominence. 'The truth of the matter,' she said in late 1974, 'is that Charles and I have contributed exactly $1,167 to the Republican party in the last four years—and only $307 of that went to national campaigns. There's no political pay-off.' (Not for money, at least, but her volunteer time and efforts on behalf of her party were certainly partly rewarded in her appointments to government posts.)

Beyond those particular items, 'money is not of great interest to me', she insisted. 'Oh, I like to see things turn out successfully. That is the creative part of business. I'm interested to see that something I'm involved with doesn't fail. But my money is managed by a bank's trust officers, although I like to be knowledgable about what is going on with it. I don't like to be left out of those decisions.'

In the spring of 1975 the Independent Broadcasting Authority that regulates ITV (Britain's independent television network) decided that Shirley Temple films 'have no relevance to modern children' and would not be shown during the network's 'children's hour'. 'We felt they were just too sentimental and mawkish to interest today's sophisticated children,' said a spokesman for the Authority. 'It was felt that Shirley Temple singing *On the Good Ship Lollipop* or *Animal Crackers in My Soup* had no relevance today. Her films are more likely to appeal to the nostalgia of older people.' And the inference was that they could be shown in other time periods than the children's.

Shirley herself had long since arrived at more or less the

same conclusion. 'We have twenty-two prints of my old films out back in the toolshed in Woodside,' she said. 'Sometimes my son used to dust them off and show them to his friends. At first I thought they regarded them as high camp, but they really seemed to enjoy them.' She never watched her films in their frequent television re-runs. In fact, her only viewing of anyone's motion pictures in the 1960s and 1970s was 'on aeroplanes, and I'm not sure I'm a good judge. I fell asleep during *The Sting* and it won an Academy Award. I also fell asleep when I saw *The French Connection* on a plane. And that won the Academy Award. Maybe when I fall asleep in a movie it's a good sign.'

In 1972 Shirley put away the last of her childish things; with her own daughters fully grown, she gave her doll collection to the Stanford Children's Hospital, where at any given time about five hundred of her dolls are on display in the reception area. She kept several Shirley Temple mugs, cereal bowls and cream pitchers but proceded to wash them in the dishwasher to get her image off them. 'I love blue glass but I'm awful tired of that face,' she explained. And she no longer had Hollywood friends. 'I knew a lot of people there when I was a child,' she said, 'but most of them have gone to the Great Beyond. I was so young I wasn't really close to that many people, anyway.'

Aged forty-seven in 1975, Shirley's dimpled cheeks and dark flashing eyes were the same as they had been in the films. But the blonde curls were a long distant memory, and her very dark hair was swept back in an almost matronly hair-do. Her figure was plumpish but well-rounded on her five-foot-two frame. Uncannily, her laugh, actually part giggle, went straight back at least to *Stand Up and Cheer* in 1934, although coming from an adult mouth it sometimes seemed more nervous than spontaneous.

Living down her former self she said was 'not a problem within my circle of friends or really with anyone except a few older people who are stuck on this image of the little girl. That's their problem.' When she travelled many people recognised her right away, and her name always opened doors— 'Some have told me it's like having a distant relative visit, someone they've known all their lives.' But when she posed for a photograph with the President of the United Nations General Assembly in 1974 he said, 'Thank you very much, Miss MacLaine.' And that wasn't the only time she had been taken for the tall, red-headed Shirley MacLaine.

'For years I tried to get into Red China,' said Shirley Black, still using cold war terminology in 1974. 'I didn't think I'd have a hard time because I was one of three Americans who signed a petition asking for China's admission to the United Nations and sent it to President Nixon. When I mentioned it to Henry Kissinger he said, "Shhh, don't talk about it." I didn't know he was already preparing for China's admission. An answer to my application to get into Red China never came, but Shirley MacLaine got a letter inviting *her* to come to China. I'm sure the letter was meant for me; they got their Shirleys confused.'

One of the lessons she learned in her forties, Shirley noted, was 'never to give a definite answer—yes or no— anymore. I used to give very definite answers when I was about fifteen. At sixteen one is the oldest one ever is in life. You think you know everything. People would ask, "Are you going to do such and such?" and I'd say, "Oh, no, I'd *never* do that"— very definite and very likely untrue. So I'm very careful of that now, because I don't know where life is taking me, where any road will lead. I'd never have dreamed of working at the United Nations, which didn't even exist when I was a child, or of being an ambassador.'

Her various jobs, she claimed, just happened along. 'I

don't go looking for work. I seem to be a born volunteer and I've always been interested in people and projects. Maybe I should have been a reporter. When there is a need and I can do something about it, I am happy to do it. I am also happy to say that I've made no enemies that I know of. The only people who won't talk to me are the Albanians; but then, they won't talk to anyone else either.'

Shirley felt that everything that had happened in her life was useful and had somehow prepared her for international relations. The cast of characters had changed from the likes of Mussolini's sons and Eleanor Roosevelt, to Golda Meir and Anwar Sadat. ('She's the most fascinating woman in the world and he is the man with the most charisma,' said Shirley of the latter two. 'Now that's spoken like a true diplomat, isn't it?') But along the way she had learned to shop. ('I buy quality not quantity, because it lasts longer and is more frugal. I'm not much on high fashion; I simply can't be frivolous because I travel so much, I like to wear serious clothes.') She had learned to fly from continent to continent with only two suitcases, but always with room left over for her emergency chocolate rations. And she learned how to write her own speeches, how to get all her homework done, and how to keep from drinking too much at embassy functions.

In her own home Shirley indulged in cooking and gardening, and the garden in Woodside contained, in addition to immensely practical crops such as lettuce, potatoes and tomatoes, tiny Tahitian gardenias, her favourite flower, and trees bearing Meyer lemons. Although she had been working with the Sierra Club and the National Wildlife Federation and was, along with Charles and their children, interested in conservation and the environment she noted that 'it wasn't until Earth Day, 1970 that I really felt the environmental movement was going to play a dominant place in my life—and in that of my family'.

From that point, apart from her formal work on the national and international level, Shirley and her children began to recycle cans and newspapers. Lori worked at Sealife Park, with sea lions, porpoises, killer whales and various fish, and spent six weeks on an Outward Bound course in the Sierra Mountains, where one project was to live alone for thirty-six hours, finding water and wild food to live on. Charles Jnr was an ardent backpacker, and Susan's special outdoor love was horse riding. All of them went away to camp, a working ranch in Arizona where they raised their own animals and vegetables.

'Being all native Californians, we are naturally outdoor people,' Shirley said. 'We have a reverence for nature and we feel very strongly that people must learn to live with nature and not try to conquer it. In the past we've taken everything for granted—the fruits of the soil and so on—and now we can't take *anything* for granted. The world has awakened to the environmental problem, to the mess that we find ourselves in, and it's now a question of how we are going to live our lives, how we use our own personal energies and our natural resources that we know have limits. It can't be talk anymore, but it must be a new living ethic that affects every citizen.'

Shirley, as a tomboy in Santa Monica, had learned to fish, and she and Charles still loved to fish together, especially for steelheads in Northern California and the Pacific Northwest, on trips lasting as long as five days. 'And we eat all we catch,' she said. 'It's always peaceful, sometimes exciting and I find these trips relaxing.' Charles, as President of Mardela International, worked in aquaculture among such diverse groups as the Lummi and Paiute Indians in North America, and with the Yugoslavian government.

Charles taught countries to catch more and better fish and

to set up cold storage places for fish. He taught the Lummis to raise Belgian oysters and to 'grow' strong domestic trout. In a two-year project with Yugoslavia, Charles provided 'good strong American catfish for matrimony with Yugoslavian catfish', as Shirley delicately put it. 'Charlie designed the shipping boxes and sent some 180,000 catfish over to Yugoslavia, where catfish are considered to be quite a delicacy and sell for the equivalent of $1.50 a pound. His main love has always been the ocean and fish and he has this unique ability to combine business with fish. He is a Pisces. I'm a Taurus, a worrier. Taurus people find out quickly who they can trust.' She felt that the real strength of their relationship was that 'my husband and I are both on our own courses, but they're complementary. You can't just have love, which is the most important thing, you must also have interests that are somewhat the same.'

Shirley considered that most of her life had been 'free from stumbling blocks', and never liked to dwell on problems, her own or anyone else's—'I want to know what's going to happen tomorrow', she was fond of saying. But what happened to Shirley Temple Black in the autumn of 1972 was a problem that had to be dealt with immediately and head on : cancer of the breast. The American Cancer Society said it was a problem for seven out of one hundred women, and Shirley, after thinking, 'Oh God, why is this happening to me', decided to share the experience of her mastectomy publicly, and became the first well-known woman to do so. 'Maybe that was the reason it happened to me,' she said, 'so I could tell the women of the world, who are my sisters, that they should go to the doctor for diagnosis when they have unusual symptoms, and that they should learn to examine themselves.'

She discovered the lump on her left breast herself, in September 1972 in Washington D.C. 'As soon as I got home to California I called my doctor and he gave me a mammography, which is an X-ray of the breast, and decided I should have a biopsy to see whether the tumour was benign or malignant. He said my chances were about sixty to forty, which I thought were pretty good odds.' Between Shirley's schedule and the doctor's it was 1 November before she entered the hospital and 2 November before the biopsy was performed.

'I wouldn't let them go any further,' she said. 'I only signed the release to let them do the biopsy. I said, "Doctor, you make the incision and I'll make the decision." Because it's my body. I have the right to decide what happens to that body. I think if the cancer had metastasised, spread all over my body, maybe I would choose not to have any surgery at all.'

This was unusual, since if the tumour turned out to be malignant doctors preferred to perform the mastectomy right away rather than put the patient through two separate anaesthetics and operations. But Shirley recalled a girlfriend of hers who went to the hospital, didn't pay too much attention to what she was signing and woke up without a breast.

Nevertheless, when Shirley woke up from her biopsy the doctor, with Charles's help, told her that the tumour was removed but that it had been malignant and a mastectomy would have to be performed. 'After I fully recovered from the anaesthetic I had a good cry over the whole thing,' Shirley recalled 'and my daughters came to the hospital and we all cried for a while. When that was over I decided that we would go ahead with the operation, a modified radical mastectomy, which is the removal of the breast and some lymph nodes in the armpit—twelve nodes out of about eighty in the armpit.'

The tumour itself had been only two centimetres in length, and the malignant part was no bigger than the tip of Shirley's fingernail. 'The decision to have the operation wasn't too difficult to make,' said Shirley, 'since the alternative was to die. The operation is an ugly operation and it is a maiming operation, and it takes a while to get used to your revised body, so I don't want to be too light about the subject or mislead anyone.' Still, with characteristic dedication, Shirley did a Dinah Shore TV talk show just two days before the operation—'We both put on seven pounds that day, eating Russian food until it came out of our ears', Dinah recalled—and three days after the operation Shirley announced it to the world. Within a month she was back at work with the Council on Environmental Quality.

'The first time I came out of the anaesthetic I said "seabed",' Shirley remembered, 'and Charlie said, "You're still at that meeting in Geneva". I went back to sleep and the second time I came to I said "chocolate". Now that's the real me. Susan was sitting by my bed and she went out and bought some of those little chocolate kisses. There is probably quite a bit of depression after any operation because of the anaesthetic and the shock to your system. What I did was cry when I felt like crying, even in front of the children. Some people suggest that you should go cry alone so that you don't depress your family but I think you have to be yourself: when you feel unhappy, let everybody know it so long as you don't carry it to the extreme.'

Shirley's room in the hospital 'looked like a gangster's funeral', and within a few hours she was walking around the halls like Lady Bountiful, dispensing floral tributes to those patients who had fewer than she. Reporters and admirers dressed up as nurses and attendants, trying to sneak into her room, but Lori and Susan took turns standing guard during the day and Charles rolled a cot into the room to stay with Shirley at night. During the two days after the operation Shirley discussed with the three of them the possibility of making the mastectomy public 'to get the words cancer and removal of a breast talked about'. Charles Jnr was on a fishing boat off Panama but fortunately called in and agreed with the others that Mom should speak out.

Accordingly, Shirley went on radio and television and wrote an article on the whole experience in the February 1973 *McCall's*, which elicited more than fifty-thousand letters from people who had had or were contemplating mastectomies—including three men. 'I don't think there's anything worse than talking about your operation,' she said. 'But I did want to urge all women to have check-ups and to check themselves, because the whole thing came as quite a surprise to me, a very unpleasant shock. I got one very interesting letter from a woman in Oakland who said she had been slightly offended to see that I was describing in a magazine how I had my breast removed, but that same evening while she was showering she had found a lump in her own breast. She was writing from the hospital having just had a mastectomy, and she was grateful. That alone made my writing about it worthwhile.'

There were adjustments to be made. ('As soon as I learned how to pronounce "prosthesis" I went out and bought one.') Three weeks after surgery Shirley made a speech on the environment, in Chicago, that she had committed herself to six months previously. 'I had three silk scarves to wear, all sentimental,' she recalled. 'One I had worn when I met President Roosevelt, and during my speech one of my scarves came out. I felt like Sally Rand.'

While it usually takes five years to be sure the cancer won't recur, Shirley was pronounced cured, and assured she could resume a full work schedule. 'I'm grateful to God, my family and the doctors,' she said at the time, 'because I have much more to accomplish before I'm through.' Charles, she noted later, hadn't 'changed since the operation. Our love is very strong. We looked at the problem without shame and directly, and well, he's just my life. We're going along as normal. I don't think that people should think about changing after an operation of this sort. I think if you had a good husband before, he'll be a good husband. If you had a rotten husband before I really don't think he's going to change. And if you have a good marriage, nothing is really going to hurt it.'

Chapter Twelve

In the late spring and early summer of 1974 Shirley was, by her own reckoning, 'a woman of leisure'. In May she became the first woman to be appointed to the board of directors of Walt Disney Productions—'Window dressing', a Disney executive conceded. And that, despite her ongoing membership in the Screen Actors' Guild, was as much involvement with the film industry as she ever wanted again. 'I have been a union member for forty-three years', she noted, 'and now I think it's time they gave me a testimonial dinner and a gold watch.'

The name Shirley Temple Black, and the person, now appeared as a director on the boards of Disney, Del Monte (Foods) Corporation, the United States Association for the United Nations, the National Wildlife Federation and the National Multiple Sclerosis Society. In addition Shirley was doing volunteer work with the U.N.'s Food and Agriculture Organisation, and was a member of the U.S. Commission for UNESCO. But as she put it, succinctly and typically, since her resignation from the President's Council on Environmental Quality in January, she had been 'keeping busy but with no salary coming in'. She wanted and was ready for a full-time job. Her physical condition, a year and a half after the mastectomy, was of no concern to her : 'My health was great before my operation for breast cancer, and it's been great ever since,' she said. 'It's just that in between I lost an old friend.'

There were recurring rumours in Washington and New York that Shirley Temple Black was about to be appointed by Nixon to a diplomatic post in sub-Sahara Africa. She heard the talk, too, and with her consuming interest in the third world it seemed to her an appropriate step. One night, at a state dinner at the White House, she sidled over to Secretary of State Henry Kissinger and said, 'I hear a rumour that I'm going to Africa.' Shirley later recalled Kissinger's saying, 'It's not a rumour—it's a fact; and do you know why I'm sending you? Because several years ago you attended a White House briefing and asked me about Namibia. I still knew the country by its old name : South-west Africa.' And she added : 'He was very impressed with my knowledge and never forgot that moment.'

But even though the post of Ambassador to Ghana was already vacant, Shirley's appointment was held up, along with several others, for a few months while Nixon devoted nearly all of his energies to holding on to the presidency in the wake of the Watergate scandals. Shirley knew of her upcoming nomination but couldn't talk about it except with the family. It was only in August 1974, after Nixon was forced to resign and Vice-President Gerald Ford replaced him—and reapproved the Black posting—that Shirley's designation became official.

The Ghanaian government was so excited about the new U.S. Ambassador-designate that Accra jumped the gun on Washington by four days, announcing Shirley's appointment on Thursday, 16 August. Charles and Shirley were wisely away from Woodside on a long weekend, and Charles Jnr and others who answered the phone at home referred callers to Mrs Black on her return Monday morning. The State Department in Washington refused to confirm the report from Ghana but added that they had no reason to deny it. On Monday 20 August, both the American government and Shirley Temple Black confirmed the news, and the reactions to it were widely varied.

She herself saw the nomination 'in the logical progression of jobs I've had since I retired from the movies', although despite her extensive world travels, Shirley had never been to Ghana, nor to anywhere else in Africa except Egypt, where, on one of her three visits, Egyptian President Anwar Sadat had told her that *Heidi* was one of his favourite films. She had two books in the library at Woodside to help her in a quick study before the U.S. Senate had to confirm her appointment: They were *Africa: Images and Realities*, a picture book, and *West African Travels: A Guide to People and Places*. Shirley read in the encyclopedia that Ghana, a country of only nine million persons, exports most of the world's cocoa. 'I just love chocolate but I'd better keep my knowledge, such as it is, to myself,' she giggled. 'I don't know how the Senate will like this kind of enthusiasm.'

Yale University Professor David Apter, a leading U.S. authority on Ghana and author of *Ghana in Transition*, a basic text on West African politics, was not amused by the nomination. 'It's an insult to Ghana, a slap in the face, irrelevant and outrageous,' he said. 'The post calls for a career foreign service officer or an experienced diplomat, someone who understands the country's historic ties to the aspirations of American blacks, and who understands Ghana's symbolic importance as the first African colony to gain independence after World War II, and as a leader of pan-Africanism.' Apter dispatched a telegram of protest to Kissinger.

However, Franklin Williams, a black who had served as U.S. Ambassador to Ghana under President Lyndon Johnson, predicted that Shirley would 'prove to be a sensitive, warm and capable ambassador'. Another male former envoy to Ghana, who requested anonymity, observed in Shirley's defence that 'half the career foreign service people I've met were fine public servants, but the other half were horses' asses. Being a career diplomat is not what's important; if she gets a good deputy chief of mission I think she'll be a smash.'

Mindful of the necessity of keeping a discreet silence on the specifics of the Ambassador's role in Ghana before she was confirmed, Shirley cited as proof of her fitness her 'many good African friends since 1969, when I sat in alphabetical order at the United Nations General Assembly between Upper Volta on my right and the United Republic of Tanzania on my left. They evidently said good things about me when they went back home,' she said. Indeed, most ordinary citizens in Ghana didn't know of her childhood film career, but did know of her work at the U.N. A leading Ghanaian intellectual visiting the United States at the time of Shirley's appointment said his countrymen and women would be open-minded and that her most important potential qualification would be her influence in Washington. 'As a woman and a former movie star maybe people in the United States will listen to what she has to say about us,' he said. 'What's important is that she be well-disposed toward Africa and capable of providing reasonable and sensible advice to her own country.'

A high official at the State Department had warned her just before she was publicly named as Ambassador to expect some adverse reaction in the United States. 'We know what you can do and the other countries know what you can do but most American journalists and the general public aren't aware that you're capable of these assignments,' he said. Shirley added at the time, 'I know me. I know how I feel and I feel a kinship with all human beings. It's just that I can't say I feel capable because I don't want to have that quoted before the Senate Hearings.'

Awaiting the U.S. Senate Hearings on her confirmation Shirley spent her time 'mostly reading and thinking' about this latest role she'd been offered, and about the little country more than 7,500 miles from Woodside that she hadn't yet seen. She recalled Eleanor Roosevelt, whom she had first met on the set of *Little Miss Broadway* in 1937, and whose husband Franklin had given the little girl credit for getting America through the Depression. 'I see a link between Mrs Roosevelt's later years and my own recent activities,' Shirley said. 'A lot of her work in international affairs has got to me by osmosis and been an inspiration to me at the United Nations and in the five years since.'

That might seem like heresy for the lifelong 'Republican but Independent' whose devotion to her political party had ranged from stuffing envelopes and walking precincts to running for Congress and giving speeches for free, and had resulted in a string of what were essentially, after all, political appointments. But Shirley had an image problem from this second public career as well as from her first, in films. In her first and last try for elected office, that 1967 special primary election for the U.S. House of Representatives, she had been unfairly lumped with Ronald Reagan and George Murphy in the right-wing, ex-actor school of California politics. 'Really I'm a fiscal conservative, liberal to moderate on domestic issues, and very liberal internationally,' she reminded a visitor. 'People don't realise what I've been doing all these years,' she complained. 'Even now when I'm at home, some friends still think I'm at the U.N.'

Her chief concern in the days following her appointment was the lack of sufficient protein in developing countries. 'The food crisis is going to make the energy crisis pale by comparison, even in the affluent nations,' she predicted, noting that the price of poultry feed had increased from $150 to $600 a ton in less than three years, making eggs and chickens, two primary sources of protein, prohibitive to the developing world. And she and Charles shared a concern over "the disparity of fishing habits around the globe'. She pointed out, 'Forty nations fish off the West Coast of Africa, but the people in the raging drought areas of Central Africa aren't getting any of that fish. Yet the yield of the Indian Ocean could increase five times over.'

The U.S. Senate, perhaps sensing that Shirley's people-to-people ambassadorship might be more effective at that time in the history of the United States and Ghana than one based on a sounder intellectual record, and certainly weary of the Watergate mess and the consequent mass distrust of professional politicians, swiftly—and unanimously—confirmed Shirley Temple Black as U.S. envoy to Ghana. Her confirmation on 12 September 1974, and those of former Kentucky Senator John Sherman Cooper as the first U.S. Ambassador to East Germany, and of former presidential economic adviser Kenneth Rush as ambassador to France, gave the Ford administration its first three diplomatic appointments.

In the next two and a half months Shirley had fifty-five official State Department briefings on Ghana and United States diplomacy—'and Lord knows how many unofficial ones', she recalled. 'The State Department made me feel as though I'd already served in Ghana and was ready for a new assignment. But at least I felt confident when I got to Accra.' She also talked with professors of economics, political science and sociology, and businessmen whose firms had large investments in Ghana. She took a crash brush-up course in French and read books and documents in her most conscientious 'one-take Temple' style. Shirley, Charles and Susan—who were to accompany her to Ghana, leaving Charles Jnr and Lori at home to finish university, each had several vaccinations against exotic near-equatorial diseases. At the last Washington meeting with Kissinger, he promised to visit her in late 1975. 'With any luck I'll still be there,' she joked to the Secretary of State. 'You won't have recalled me and I'll be serving.'

On 29 November 1974, Shirley took a wistful look around the Woodside house and drove with the family up to the San Francisco airport, where she left behind the life of a California suburban matron for her posting in sweltering sub-Sahara Africa. Although Shirley's predecessor in Accra, Fred L. Hadsell, had held his job for three years, and she might be in Ghana even longer, it never occurred to her and Charles to sell the Woodside house. Shirley's parting shot to Charles Jnr was, 'Don't take off that moustache, I'm gettin' to like it.' And to newsmen who followed her to the aeroplane she confided that she had turned down several European diplomatic posts—not necessarily at the ambassadorial level—and a job as an agency head in Washington, in order to go exactly where she was headed today. 'If I could have picked a place to serve it would have been in black Africa,' she asserted.

The Ghana she arrived in the next day was suffering from rampant inflation worsened by quadrupled world oil prices; a shortage of investment capital from abroad; and a stagnant agriculture. None of these was visible as Shirley, Charles and Susan stepped off the plane in Accra, and all was temporarily forgotten in the warmth of welcome in English—or 'Awwaaba' in the Twi tribal language. Men in the tropical worsted suits that are one of the legacies of English colonialism and men and women in garments of colourful local cotton cloth waved and shouted to Madam Ambassador and her family. Ghana, once a prime shipping point for slaves going to America, was considered one of the friendliest nations in

Africa. Although its government was a military dictatorship, there was a minimum of bureaucracy and there were few overt trappings of a police state. Its Twi, Ga and Shanti tribes were open, hospitable and confident.

As a successful career woman, Ambassador Black had been ideally selected for Ghana, where women's liberation slogans were found even in the most remote villages. And as a long-term and outspoken opponent of racial separation in a country vocally and vigorously involved in supporting African liberation movements all over the continent, Shirley was championed by both men and women from the instant of her arrival. She quickly became one of Ghana's 'wanto wazuri', which in Ashanti means 'beautiful people'.

Four days after her arrival Shirley presented her credentials to the Ghanaian head of state, Colonel Ignatius Acheampong, leader of the country's ruling military junta, in the stately sort of princess-comes-to-the-palace ceremony she had loved since childhood. In fact, the presentation of credentials ceremony was worthy both of the former Gold Coast's British background and Shirley's Hollywood one. 'It was probably the most thrilling moment of my life,' she said. 'Standing alone in a little canopied setting with the Ghanaian Air Force band playing *The Star Spangled Banner* was almost too much. I was covered in gooseflesh. Then the talking drums of welcome really covered me with gooseflesh; the talking drums go all the way to the pit of your stomach. To me it was like the pages of *The National Geographic* magazine come to life.'

She stepped forward from her canopy and presented a leather portfolio from Washington to Colonel Acheampong, and in a strong clear voice with the tight accent of her native California she said : 'Your excellency, I am deeply honoured to present the letters by which the President of the United States Gerald R. Ford accredits me as ambassador extraordinary and plenipotentiary of the United States of America to the Republic of Ghana. Thank you.' And Shirley Temple Black was now 'Her Excellency' and ready to go to work.

Acheampong impressed her as ' a serious hardworking and determined man of vision'. Shirley visited Kumasi in Ghana's central region and called on the country's most important tribal chief, Otumfuo Opoku II, the Asantehen of the Ashanti tribe. Her first stop at a rural outhouse gave her no cause to hesitate; since it was no worse than those on many film locations. 'The first one of these I was ever in I was three years old,' she noted. 'Problems of this nature are never problems to rugged Californians.' She further suggested that one of the six cubicles have her name on it: 'One for the ambassador'.

The ambassador's residence she shared with Charles and Susan in Accra was comfortable and well-staffed without being the country club that many embassies are, even in developing nations. 'Charlie's on the road a lot,' she explained several months into her residency, 'advising many countries how to improve their commercial fishing resources. But he can't work in Ghana since I'm the ambassador and that might pose a conflict of interest. He gets back here often enough for us to have a good home life.

'Susan roams around the country, visiting villages and attending durbars (official receptions). She's already had her first article accepted by the Burlingame paper back in California, so she's a bonafide foreign correspondent now,' beamed a proud mother.

Shirley's own trips to villages in the interior of Ghana from Accra on the coast were frequent, happy and noisy, as dozens of villagers greeted her at every stop. She flashed the dimples and smiled, suggested to one expectant mother that she name a daughter—should she have one—Shirley, and tried to meet as many Ghanaians as she could, greeting each in a few words of his or her tribal language as well as in English, the country's official tongue. The shots she and the American members of her household had taken back home successfully immunised them from disease, although they continued to take anti-malaria pills once a week. 'In Ghana we have a variety of malaria that is quickly fatal,' she explained, 'and we must remember our every-Sunday ritual: malaria tablets with breakfast.'

Less than half a year into her stint as U.S. Ambassador to Ghana Shirley was winning more raves from Ghanaians— few of whom were concerned with her prior lives—than she had ever won from critics during her first career. The government decided to put her face on a coin, making her only the fourth woman to be so honoured by Ghana. The others were Queen Elizabeth, Indira Ghandi and Coretta King, the widow of Martin Luther King Jnr.

She astonished the professional diplomats in her embassy by appearing for work in brightly printed cotton gowns, often of orange, green and brown with matching head-scarves, of the sort favoured by local women, and wearing earrings and bracelets of Ghanaian gold. With her gift for mimicry and languages she took to using native phrases, such as the welcoming 'awwaabe' and 'oyiwala donn' ('thank you' in Ga) in both official and informal conversation. She acquired a boxer puppy and dubbed him 'ma danfo' ('my friend' in Twi).

Occasionally, Shirley was mistaken for an actual American black, thanks to her Californian-based suntan, burnished and deepened by the west African sun, and her dark hair and eyes. And the ambassador was glad that her child star days were only dimly known in Ghana and that somebody somewhere had missed her films. She was plainly tired of the foreign press in Ghana calling her a 'former child star'. 'Dr

Kissinger was a former child, Jerry Ford was a former child, even F.D.R. was a former child,' she snapped, the dimples flashing to soften the pique. 'I retired from the movies in 1949 but I'm still a former child.' She laughed at her own anger, and said more seriously, 'I'm delighted at last to be thought of as a diplomat rather than as a film entertainer.'

Still the film pro's instincts were intact. On a visit to the Accra Polytechnic School, an event heavily photographed by television news teams, Shirley stepped from her limousine, tripped and stumbled—the cameras whirring the whole time. Her dancer's reflexes kept her from hitting the ground but the newsmen stood silent. The nervous giggle erupted from Shirley and, in a smiling gesture reminiscent of that little girl who used to hold up her hand to spoil what she knew was a bad take, she said, 'Wow, I blew it. Let's do that one over, boys.' And the lady ambassador walked through another take, just as the little girl would have done.

Shirley's greatest triumph of ambassadorial choreography was with Accra's Market Women's Association, who run nine per cent of the country's stalls and shops and most of its fishing boats. These 'market mammies', who tend to physical hugeness to symbolise their vast commercial wealth and power, invited Shirley to visit the colourful outdoor Macoola market, where she embraced them as sister working girls.

'It was an exciting and heartwarming experience,' she recalled. 'They were all wearing local cloth and singing songs of welcome; they spread cloth on the ground in front of me. I didn't want to step on it until they explained it was a sign of welcome. So I stood on the cloth and did a Highlife in my walking shoes.' She spoke of the wriggling national dance as 'not hard to learn'. 'The music is complicated but the step itself is easy. The women seemed pleased that the United States has a lady ambassador here,' she noted. 'They like a woman with political strength.'

Although she noted that 'there are no major problems in U.S.-Ghana relations and the feelings are good', there were problems in Ghana in 1975 that engaged her concern: the country's unsuccessful quest for its own oil in view of world oil prices, worldwide inflation and debts left over from the régime of Kwame Nkrumah. One hopeful note was the success of the government's 'operation feed yourself' programme to reduce Ghana's dependence on imports. 'My job is to stimulate American action here,' she said, 'and to look after the interests of my country in trade and diplomacy in Ghana. I'd like to see more done in terms of health assistance, particularly maternal child care, and in trying to encourage U.S. business interests to get involved.'

At first she worked the embassy staff very hard, easing up a little after the first three months and then insisting only on fortnightly meetings instead of the weekly ones she had held at first. One of her subordinates termed her 'easy to work with, very understanding, a thorough professional'. 'I work a seventeen-hour day and I'm personally responsible for 108 staff members in the embassy,' she said. 'If anything goes wrong I'm to blame. And if there were sudden developments I'd have to make split-second decisions and they'd have to be the right ones. It's a tremendous work load but I have no regrets. I've not been bored for an instant. My biggest problem is that I rise at 6 am and work steadily all day. At night there is almost always an official function that I must attend. And in Ghana everyone eats late, dinner seldom starts before 9 pm. I get very little sleep but I still feel so robust I sometimes wear everybody else out.'

It seemed to Shirley that, 'Everything I've done in my life has directed me to this kind of job. Little Shirley opened a lot of doors for me, and we all learn a lot from the past—it's just that we shouldn't live there. I don't want to sit in a lovely house and look at old scrapbooks. I like to work. If my ambas-

sador days come to an end, I think I would return to some
kind of work at the United Nations. But I'll never make
another movie, those days are over. I loved my life as a child.
But this I find much harder work. There's no ending to the
stories : it's not like having a script where it all works out
neatly.'

Appendix

Shirley Temple's Movies

1932

BABY BURLESKS, Educational Films (all one reel)
1. War Babies*
2. The Runt Page*
3. Pie Covered Wagon*
4. Glad Rags to Riches*

Feature Film

5. THE RED-HAIRED ALIBI, Capital Films; Director, Christy Cabanne; based on the novel by Wilson Collison. Cast included: Merna Kennedy, Theodore von Eltz, Grant Withers.

1933

BABY BURLESKS, Educational Films (all one reel)
6. Kid's Last Fight*
7. Kid 'n' Hollywood*
8. Polly-tix in Washington*

9. Kid 'n' Africa*
FROLICS OF YOUTH, Educational (two reels)
10. Merrily Yours*
ANDY CLYDE SERIES Educational (two reels)
11. Dora's Dunkin' Donuts*

Feature Films

12. TO THE LAST MAN, Paramount; Director, Henry Hathaway; Screenplay by Jack Cunningham, based on the novel by Zane Grey. Cast included: Randolph Scott, Jack LaRue, Esther Ralston, Buster Crabbe, Noah Beery.
13. OUT ALL NIGHT, Universal; Sam Taylor; William Anthony McGuire, based on a story by Tim Whalen. Cast included: Slim Summerville, Zasu Pitts.

1934

FROLICS OF YOUTH, Educational (two reels)
14. Pardon My Pups*
15. Managed Money*
Musical Featurette, Paramount
16. New Deal Rhythm

Feature Films

17. CAROLINA, Fox; Henry King; Reginald Berkeley, based on the Paul Green play *The House of Connelly*. Cast: Janet Gaynor, Lionel Barrymore, Robert Young, Stepin Fetchit.
18. MANDALAY, Warner Brothers-First National; Michael Curtiz; Austin Parker and Charles Kenyon, based on a story by Paul Hervey Fox. Cast: Kay Francis, Ricardo Cortez, Warner Oland, Lyle Talbot.
19. STAND UP AND CHEER, Fox; Hamilton McFadden; Ralph Spence, based on a story outline by Will Rogers and Philip

* Educational Films were all produced by Jack Hays and directed by Charles Lamont.

147

Klein; songs by Lew Brown, Jay Gorney (including *Baby, Take A Bow*). Cast: Warner Baxter, Madge Evans, Nigel Bruce, Stepin Fetchit.

20. NOW I'LL TELL, Fox; Edwin Burke; Burke, based on the book by Mrs Arnold Rothstein. Cast: Spencer Tracy, Helen Twelvetrees, Alice Faye.

21. CHANGE OF HEART, Fox; John G. Blystone; Sonya Levien, based on the novel by Kathleen Norris. Cast: Janet Gaynor, Charles Farrell, Ginger Rogers.

22. LITTLE MISS MARKER, Paramount; Alexander Hall; William R. Lipman, Sam Hellman, Gladys Lehman, based on the story by Damon Runyon. Cast: Adolphe Menjou, Dorothy Dell, Charles Bickford.

23. BABY, TAKE A BOW, Fox; Harry Lachman; Philip Klein and E. E. Paramore Jnr, based on the play *Square Crooks* by James P. Judge. Cast: James Dunn, Claire Trevor.

24. NOW AND FOREVER, Paramount; Henry Hathaway; Vincent Lawrence and Sylvia Thalberg, based on the story by Jack Kirkland and Melville Baker. Cast: Gary Cooper, Carole Lombard.

25. BRIGHT EYES, Fox; David Butler; William Conselman, based on a story by Butler, Edwin Burke; song (*On the Good Ship Lollipop*) Sidney Clare, Richard Whiting. Cast: James Dunn, Judith Allen, Lois Wilson, Jane Withers, Jane Darwell.

1935
All Twentieth Century-Fox

26. THE LITTLE COLONEL, David Butler; William Conselman, based on the story by Annie Fellows Johnston. Cast: Lionel Barrymore, Evelyn Venable, John Lodge, Bill Robinson, Hattie McDaniel.

27. OUR LITTLE GIRL, John Robertson; Stephen Avery, Allen

Rivkin, Jack Yellen, based on the story *Heaven's Gate* by Florence Leighton Pfalzgraf; song, Paul Francis Webster, Lew Pollack. Cast: Rosemary Ames, Joel McCrea, Lyle Talbot.

28. CURLY TOP, Irving Cummings; Patterson McNutt, Arthur Beckhard, based on the novel by Jean Webster; songs by Ray Henderson, Ted Koehler, Edward Heyman, Irving Caesar (including *Animal Crackers, It's All So New to Me, When I Grow Up, The Simple Things, Curly Top*). Cast: John Boles, Rochelle Hudson, Jane Darwell, Arthur Treacher.

29. THE LITTLEST REBEL, David Butler; Edwin Burke, based on the play by Edward Peple. Cast: John Boles, Jack Holt, Karen Morley, Bill Robinson.

1936
All Twentieth Century-Fox

30. CAPTAIN JANUARY, David Butler; Sam Hellman, Gladys Lehman, Harry Tugend, based on the story by Laura E. Richards; songs by Lew Pollack, Sidney D. Mitchell, Jack Yellen (including *Early Bird, At the Codfish Ball, The Right Somebody to Love*). Cast: Guy Kibbee, Slim Summerville, Buddy Ebsen, Jane Darwell.

31. POOR LITTLE RICH GIRL, Irving Cummings; Sam Hellman, Gladys Lehman, Harry Tugend, based on stories by Eleanor Gates; songs by Mack Gordon, Harry Revel (including *But Definitely; You've Got to Eat Your Spinach, Baby; When I'm With You*). Cast: Alice Faye, Jack Haley, Gloria Stuart, Jane Darwell.

32. DIMPLES, William A. Seiter; Arthur Sheekman and Nat Perrin; songs Jimmy McHugh, Ted Koehler (including *He Was a Dandy and She Was a Belle* and *Get on Board*). Cast: Frank Morgan, Helen Westley.

33. STOWAWAY, William A. Seiter; William Conselman, Arthur Sheekman, Nat Perrin, based on the story by Sam Engel; songs by Mack Gordon, Harry Revel, Irving Caesar (including *Goodnight, My Love, You Gotta S-M-I-L-E, One Never Knows, Does One?, That's What I Want for Christmas*). Cast : Robert Young, Alice Faye, Helen Westley, Arthur Treacher.

1937
Both Twentieth Century-Fox

34. WEE WILLIE WINKLE, John Ford; Ernest Pascal and Julien Josephson, based on the story by Rudyard Kipling. Cast : Victor McLaglen, C. Aubrey Smith, Cesar Romero, Constance Collier.

35. HEIDI, Allan Dwan; Walter Ferris and Julian Josephson, based on the novel by Johanna Spyri. Cast : Jean Hersholt, Arthur Treacher, Helen Westley.

1938
All Twentieth Century-Fox

36. REBECCA OF SUNNYBROOK FARM, Allan Dwan; Karl Tunberg, Don Ettlinger, based on the novel by Kate Douglas Wiggin; songs by Sidney Mitchell and Lew Pollack, Mack Gordon and Harry Revel, Jack Yellen and Samuel Pokrass (including *Alone With You, If I Had One Wish to Make, Come and Get Your Happiness*). Cast : Randolph Scott, Jack Haley, Gloria Stuart, Helen Westley, Slim Summerville, Bill Robinson.

37. LITTLE MISS BROADWAY, Irving Cummings; Harry Tugend, Jack Yellen; songs, Walter Bullock, Harold Spina (including *Be Optimistic, How Can I Thank You, We Should Be Together*). Cast : George Murphy, Jimmy Durante, Phyllis Brooks, Edna May Oliver.

38. JUST AROUND THE CORNER, Irving Cummings; Ethel Hill, J. P. McEvoy, Darrel Ware, based on the novel *Lucky Penny* by Paul Gerard Smith. Cast : Charles Farrell, Joan Davis, Bill Robinson, Burt Lahr, Franklin Pangborn.

1939
Both Twentieth Century-Fox

39. THE LITTLE PRINCESS, Walter Lang; Ethel Hill, Walter Ferris, based on the novel by Frances Hodgson Burnett. Cast : Richard Green, Anita Louise, Ian Hunter, Cesar Romero, Arthur Treacher. Filmed in colour.

40. SUSANNAH OF THE MOUNTIES, William A. Seiter; Robert Ellis and Helen Logan, based on the story by Fidel La Barba and Walter Ferris and the book by Muriel Denison. Cast : Randolph Scott, Margaret Lockwood, Martin Good Rider, J. Farrell Mac Donald.

1940
Both Twentieth Century-Fox

41. THE BLUE BIRD, Walter Lang; Ernest Pascal, based on the play by Maurice Maeterlinck. Cast : Spring Byington, Nigel Bruce, Gale Sondergaard. Filmed in colour.

42. YOUNG PEOPLE, Allan Dwan; Edwin Blum, Don Ettlinger; songs Mack Gordon, Harry Warren (including *Strolling on the Avenue, I Wouldn't Take a Million*). Cast : Jack Oakie, Charlotte Greenwood, George Montgomery, Mae Marsh.

1941

43. KATHLEEN, Metro-Goldwyn-Mayer; Harold S. Bucquet;

Mary McCall Jnr, based on the story by Kay Van Riper. Cast: Laraine Day, Herbert Marshall, Gail Patrick.

1942

44. MISS ANNIE ROONEY, United Artists; Edward L. Marin; George Bruce. Cast: William Gargan, Guy Kibbee, Dickie Moore, June Lockhart.

1944

45. SINCE YOU WENT AWAY, David O. Selznick-United Artists; John Cromwell; Selznick, based on the novel by Margaret Buell Wilder. Cast: Claudette Colbert, Jennifer Jones, Joseph Cotten, Monty Woolley, Lionel Barrymore, Robert Walker, Agnes Moorehead, Hattie McDaniel, Guy Madison, Craig Stevens, Keenan Wynn.

46. I'LL BE SEEING YOU, David O. Selznick-United Artists; William Dieterle; Marion Parsonnet, based on the radio play by Charles Martin. Cast: Ginger Rogers, Joseph Cotten, Spring Byington, Tom Tully, Chill Wills.

1945

47. KISS AND TELL, Columbia; Richard Wallace; F. Hugh Herbert, based on his own play. Cast: Jerome Courtland, Walter Abel, Katharine Alexander, Robert Benchley, Tom Tully, Darryl Hickman.

1947

48. HONEYMOON, RKO; Willain Keighley; Michael Kanin, based on a story by Vicki Baum. Cast: Franchot Tone, Guy Madison, Lina Romay, Gene Lockhart.

49. THE BACHELOR AND THE BOBBY-SOXER, RKO; Irving Reis; Sidney Sheldon. Cast: Myrna Loy, Cary Grant, Rudy Vallee, Ray Collins.

50. THAT HAGEN GIRL, Warner Brothers; Peter Godfrey; Charles Hoffman, based on the novel by Edith Kneipple Roberts. Cast: Ronald Reagan, Rory Calhoun, Lois Maxwell, Dorothy Peterson, Charles Kemper, Conrad Janis, Penny Edwards.

1948

51. FORT APACHE, RKO; John Ford; Frank Nugent, based on the novel *Massacre* by James Warner Bellah. Cast: John Wayne, Henry Fonda, John Agar, Pedro Armendariz, Ward Bond.

1949

52. MR. BELVEDERE GOES TO COLLEGE, Twentieth Century-Fox; Elliot Nugent; Richard Sale, Mary Loos and Mary McCall Jnr, based on characters created by Gwen Davenport. Cast: Clifton Webb, Tom Drake, Alan Young, Jessie Royce Landis, Jeff Chandler.

53. ADVENTURE IN BALTIMORE, RKO; Richard Wallace, Lionel Houser, based on a story by Christopher Isherwood and Lesser Samuels. Cast: Robert Young, John Agar.

54. THE STORY OF SEABISCUIT, Warner Brothers; David Butler; John Taintor Foote, based on his own story. Cast: Barry Fitzgerald, Lon McAllister, Rosemary DeCamp.

55. A KISS FOR CORLISS, United Artists; Richard Wallace; Howard Dimsdale, based on characters created by F. Hugh Herbert. Cast: David Niven, Tom Tully, Virginia Welles, Darryl Hickman.

Index